Like Subjects, Love Objects

Like Subjects, Love Objects

Essays on Recognition and Sexual Difference

Jessica Benjamin

Yale University Press / New Haven and London

Set in Janson type by Keystone Typesetting, Inc., Orwigsburg, Pennsylvania.
Printed by Vail-Ballou Press, Binghamton, New York.

Library of Congress Cataloging-in-Publication Data
Benjamin, Jessica.
    Like subjects, love objects : essays on recognition and sexual difference / Jessica Benjamin.
        p.   cm.
    Includes bibliographical references and index.
    ISBN 0-300-06419-5 (alk. paper)
    1. Object relations (Psychoanalysis).   2. Sex differences (Psychology)   3. Psychoanalysis and feminism.   I. Title.
    [DNLM: 1. Object Attachment.   2. Psychoanalytic Theory.
    3. Gender Identity.   4. Sex Factors.   WM 460.5.02 B468L 1996]
BF175.5.024B46   1995
155.3 — dc20
DNLM/DLC
for Library of Congress   95-14346
                                                                          CIP

A catalogue record for this book is available from the British Library.

The paper in this book meets the guidelines for permanence and durability of the Committee on Production Guidelines for Book Longevity of the Council on Library Resources.

10   9   8   7   6   5   4   3   2   1

Contents

Acknowledgments

Most of the essays in this volume were first presented at an assortment of invited lectures, conferences, and seminars. They have benefited immensely from the comments of many participants at those events, too numerous to thank individually. Some of the essays, previously published, owe their genesis and present form to the encouragement and comments of previous editors. Many students over the years have helped me clarify my ideas with their thoughtful discussion of this and earlier work. My colleagues of the relational orientation at New York University Postdoctoral Psychology Program have provided me with an enlivening context for thinking and writing. The members of the Seminar on Sexual Difference and Psychoanalysis at the New York Institute for the Humanities have contributed enormously to my thinking about gender. My thanks to all of you.

I am deeply grateful for the support and criticism of a number of friends who have discussed the project of this book with me, as well as read and commented on parts of this manuscript: Lewis Aron, Fran Bartkowski, Donna Bassin, Beatrice Beebe, Muriel Dimen, Tom Domenici, Michael Eigen, Virginia Goldner, Daniel Hill, Maureen Mahoney, Zina Steinberg.

My friends at Stroemfeld Verlag in Frankfurt, in particular K. D. Wolff, helped this volume to take shape. My editors at Yale, Gladys Topkis and Dan Heaton helped to render my prose style more reader-friendly.

Finally, for their love, their merriment, and their deep understanding, as well as all they have taught me (from each, according to his abilities . . .), I thank my family: Jonah, Jake, and Andy.

Like Subjects, Love Objects

Introduction

These essays represent an effort to place in bolder relief some of the main ideas expressed in *The Bonds of Love* (1988) and to critically rethink others. I was impelled by the challenge to provide a more detailed account of the implications of my ideas for psychoanalytic theory and practice, as well as to reconsider certain problems that the intervening years have brought into focus.

The position from which I write — that of a psychoanalyst involved from the beginning with feminist thought — is not one that can rely on the well-worn grooves of an established discipline. Rather, it is located in the context of a tension between the disciplines of psychoanalysis and feminist theory. This relationship has been characterized not only by historical enmity but by divergent directions of discourse. I do not expect to synthesize or reconcile these different, only partially overlapping discourses, but I do aspire to bring them into conversation with each other, not only figuratively but literally. For some time, they have conversed in my mind, and much of what I have written is the result of this dialogue. Since I practice and teach psychoanalysis — and thereby steep myself in it every day — I hear one side more frequently and loudly. Yet the feminist movement has shaped my awareness since it captured my mind over twenty years ago. The voice that is heard in these essays is that of a psychoanalyst responding to the concerns and thoughts of my analytic colleagues while still trying to speak to the objections, criticisms, and questions of my feminist academic counterparts.

In the psychoanalytic context, a crucial factor that has shaped my thinking is the surprising development of a new openness to opposing ideas and pluralistic perspectives, a desire among different groups to join the argument, to confront their differences and consider them seriously. A broader interest in feminist ideas and discussions of gender has begun to emerge in psychoanalytic circles, and I have been asked to present my work to groups that explicitly seek to make these ideas relevant to clinical practice. The essays that follow reflect, in part, a response to such requests and to the changes in atmosphere as well as in content of psychoanalytic theory and practice in North America.

The openness to feminist ideas is doubtless connected to a significant movement within psychoanalysis. In the past fifteen years the growing interest in British Kleinian analysis and in object relations theory (called the Middle School), as well as the challenge of self psychology, with its focus on issues of narcissism and preoedipal life, have created a new context for discussion. The term *relational perspective* (Skolnick & Warshaw 1993; S. Mitchell 1993) has been used by some to describe a broad spectrum of post-Freudian positions previously identified with object relations theory.[1] These positions emphasize the internal

1. On the one hand, the term may be thought of quite generally as embodying multiple perspectives, as with *Psychoanalytic Dialogues: A Journal of Relational Perspectives*, which includes British object relations, self psychology, intersubjective theory, and interpersonal trends. However, the journal's editor, Stephen Mitchell (1988), has also used it more narrowly and specifically to designate what he calls relational-conflict perspective, which might be characterized as a mixture of Fairbairn and interpersonal currents.

representation of relations, unconscious as well as conscious, over both the classical view of instinctual conflicts and the ego psychological view of drive and defense. I am not sure whether the term *relational perspective* actually serves to define a particular segment or part of the psychoanalytic spectrum, as is often implied, or more properly characterizes a shift in thinking within (North American) psychoanalysis as a whole, which visibly affects some analysts or groups more than others. (I mention this problem of definition not because I think it so important but because it may be confusing to those outside the discipline.)

What does seem important is that many questions are now being seriously considered that previously might have been dismissed in the interests of retaining orthodoxy or group identification. In particular, the relational perspective has added to object relations theory an insistence that psychoanalysis be viewed as operating in a two-person rather than a one-person field, so that two subjectivities, each with its own set of internal relations, begin to create a new set between them. Instead of cohering in one view of the psyche — requiring a choice between, let us say, the two vastly different views of infancy proposed by self psychology and Kleinian theory — the relational perspective may best be characterized as an inquiry into questions of common concern that have come to the fore as a result of the adoption of the two-person model. So, for example, learning from and articulating the countertransference in the here-and-now relationship can be seen as a central focus by psychoanalysts with quite different notions of substantive dynamics. Agreement on the importance of the two-person field may turn out to be a rather more essential point than disagreements about the makeup of the one-person field. In many instances, this accord relegates to the background disagreements over classical metapsychology — for example, whether or not to retain Freud's theory of instincts, which often divides Europeans (who do retain it, if only metaphorically) from North Americans (who vociferously reject it).

These developments in psychoanalytic discourse have stimulated my effort to formulate psychoanalytic theory in ways that allow competing ideas to be entertained simultaneously. In contrast to seeing a sharp opposition between the drive model and the relational model, which rejects "model-mixing" (cf. S. Mitchell 1988; Greenberg and Mitchell 1983), I take eclecticism rather further than some explicit advocates of the relational perspective might (but not all: see Aron 1995). I do not see Freud's theory as something to be adopted or cast off. Rather, I think that to critique and revise his theory, to reread it and thereby change it — even radically — is our prerogative, as well as our way of being determined by it. As Foucault said in "What is an Author?" psychoanalysis represents a model of thought different from the one derived from the natural sciences, in which one thinker may simply overthrow the thinking of another. Rather, it is a discursive field, like Marxism, that is tied to its origins in certain formulations of its creators. "The work of initiators of discursivity is not situated in the space the science defines; rather it is the science, or the discursivity, which refers back to their work as the primary points of reference [coordinates]." It is necessary to "return" to the original texts because distortion and omission are intrinsic to the "act of initiation," and these barriers, which also set up "obstacles that prevent returning to the act of initiation — can only be resolved by a return" (Foucault 1977, pp. 135–137).

In other words, it is impossible not to be determined by those points of reference or primary coordinates. But if we are to avoid being wholly determined by them, we must first "return" to them; we then recognize fully the degree to which they provide the basis of our thought, even when we critique or oppose them. In fact, one is in theory more likely to be determined by a prior body of thought precisely when one thinks it can be overcome simply by rejecting its postulates. The act of rejection shapes one's starting point, and one adopts an oppositional stance that unconsciously reverses the original coordinates of the thought. To acknowledge as well as oppose this determination by a discourse is a critical form of gratitude — to kiss as well as bite the hand that feeds you. Perhaps this is a way of satisfying the need to be located in history, in tradition, without feeling that you have simply been enlisted in it: to accept that you have not created yourself without being deprived of creativity.

As to other theoretical oppositions, I have generally avoided the choice between rejecting or embracing a side, and not only because I am in favor of deconstructing such oppositions. I have too often found myself equally compelled by quite divergent accounts of the psyche from significantly different perspectives — for instance, at one point I am persuaded by the observational view that describes the infant's ability to differentiate self from mother; at another I am drawn to the clinical view that infantile experiences of agonizing, primitive fears occur at a point where loss of the other and loss of the self are indistinguishable. I have asked myself whether there is some way to remain true to that experience: reading opposing theories and finding myself drawn to both despite my awareness that each excludes something else I have found plausible or intuitively right. Quite possibly those who commit themselves wholeheartedly to one view or the other may experience a far deeper immersion in their respective positions. As for me, I arrived at the conviction that the experience of being pulled in more than one direction at once is central to my psychic life — and perhaps to many others'. In Michael Eigen's work I have more than once found a striking articulation of this ambiphilic tendency: "The Freudian baby and the Winnicottian baby are not identical. This doubleness points to the fact that no human baby is one baby. We do not know what to do with this multiplicity, but we are not free to evade it" (Eigen 1993, p. xxiii).

I have therefore tried to articulate explicitly a theme I merely suggested in *The Bonds of Love* — the nonexclusivity of the intrapsychic and intersubjective psychoanalytic models of the mind — and to explain the necessity of sustaining a kind of paradoxical tension in theory (Chapter 1; see Modell 1984; Ghent 1989). If we accept these models as distinct but not exclusive, we can preserve both views of infancy. In the essays that follow I have tried to illustrate how this tension in theory can be used — for instance, by discussing the tension between different representations of the mother, or the foregrounding of different aspects of transference. I have also argued for "overinclusiveness" (see Fast 1984), not only as a position relevant to reformulating gender complementarity but also in analyzing what ideas we make central.

Briefly, I have tried to expand on Winnicott's view that the mind works through both the relation to the other as an object of identification/projection and the relation to the other as an independent outside subject. In one of the most radical reformulations of psychoanalytic thought in this century, Winnicott (1969b) makes clear that each self may experience the other both as part of self and as an equivalent but different center of existence. The paradox is that the relation to the "inside" other may cancel or be canceled by the relation to the "outside" other; yet only when I have achieved a location between "inside" and "outside" can these terms be understood. I cannot think of one term without the other, even though I may vociferously insist that only one is relevant. What I propose throughout these essays is that both ways of being related to the other are necessary; even though each sometimes excludes the other, they can be understood as sequentially if not spatially compatible (S. Mitchell 1993). At times they coexist, and this containment of opposition simultaneously requires a kind of paradoxical stance, as when I know you to be good (in reality) because I am seeing you as bad (in fantasy), or rather because you are allowing me to see you as bad. To grasp these two relations and the theories that articulate them — intrapsychic and intersubjective — also requires a kind of transitional space in theory, which can encompass the paradoxes that arise when we are aware that two or more competing and convincing perspectives apply to the same phenomenon. At times, it is important to put aside how a particular point of view is exclusive of another, to defer the contradiction in order to entertain more than one idea.

The title *Like Subjects, Love Objects* was chosen to highlight the double-sidedness of intersubjectivity and the intrapsychic, as well as the tension between sameness and difference in gender relations. The title is meant to suggest the complex way in which each subject has to occupy simultaneously different or contrasting positions. The ambiguous term "like subjects" refers to the possibility of both recognition and identification. When we recognize the outside other as a separate and equivalent center of subjectivity, she is a "like subject." When, on the other hand, we identify with the other as inner representation, taking the other as the ideal of who we might wish to become, we also set up a relation of "like subjects."

The latter relation, which I have described elsewhere as identificatory love, may be seen as the earliest relationship of love for an outside other. Yet while it is more "outside" than the relationship of early dependency and care — traditionally devolving, therefore, on the father — it is an intrapsychic relationship to an ideal as well as an actual loving tie to another. Viewed from one angle, identification contributes to empathy and the bridging of difference. From another angle, it stands opposed to recognizing the other: the self engaged in identification takes the other as fantasy object, not as an equivalent center of being. In this sense, recognizing the other as like subject constitutes the opposite of identification, which incorporates or assimilates what is other to self. By this logic, in loving the other as an ideal "love object" the self may take a position quite inimical to inter-subjective recognition. To attribute difference to the other as sexual object, even to adore or idealize that difference, is not at all the same as to respect the other subject as an equal (Benjamin 1994).

To return for a moment to the origin of these concepts: in his remarks on narcissism, Freud (1914) proposed that we either love an other who is our source of care and protection or love someone who represents some part of ourselves that we once were, would like to be, perhaps know we cannot be. These choices correspond, respectively, to love of the anaclitic (attachment) type, which "leans on" the ego instinct, and love of the narcissistic (identificatory) type. Inasmuch as play and excitement seem to exist independent of such attachment or support, this is already a problematic bifurcation. But beyond infancy, when object love emerges not solely "leaning" on material sustenance, matters become even more complicated. Increasingly, the erotic, exciting love of the outside object comes to reflect something other than attachment; it may come closer to love of what we thought we once were or wish to be. So how do we distinguish object love from identificatory love if in object love we desire what we might have once wished to be (like) but recognize that we cannot be? And to make this distinction more difficult, does not Freud tell us that wishes never disappear — would not the prohibited identification persist and thus unconsciously unite the two aspects of love?

Here we might argue that identificatory love and outside love are two interwoven strands that intermingle in our relationships. Or instead, as I have done regarding the category "like subject," we could deconstruct the very categories by which Freud creates the opposition between object love and narcissism (see Borch-Jacobsen 1988), love of other and love of self. Then again, why not do both? My strategy is deconstructive insofar as I have engaged in a reversal (see Culler 1982) of Freud's notion that object love leads to identification — instead, showing how identification, which he once called the "earliest tie to the object" (Freud 1921), can lead to object love. However, my effort has not merely been to reverse or topple this opposition. Rather, by returning to Freud's opposition, I hope to open additional space to consider identificatory love. A strategy of critically reconstructing Freud's oppositions, recasting them from the dualism of either/or to the overinclusiveness of both/and, seems more likely to preserve the experiential basis of these categories and so to move theory more deeply into our subjective experience, clinical and otherwise.

My defense of an "overinclusive" psychoanalysis is inspired by such theoretical developments outside the psychoanalytic world as deconstruction and poststructuralism, which seek to return to the primary reference points in order to renegotiate oppositional categories. Often referred to under the rubric *postmodernism*, these tendencies in philosophy, literary critical theory, and political theory have been crucial to contemporary feminist thought and to its way of assimilating and deploying psychoanalysis.[2] It seems to me that there is a great deal for

2. Use of the term *postmodern* to characterize poststructural or deconstructionist thought and the feminist theory that works with it has encountered objections (Butler 1995). However incorrectly, these theories have nonetheless been lumped together under this rubric and discussed in relation to feminism by this term (Nicholson 1990; Benhabib 1995). There are, in fact, certain strategies of reading and conceptualizing that Americans, especially those writing literary critical theory and feminist theory, have synthesized from these rather different (mainly French) substantive trends, creating a recognizable, if by no means homogeneous, field of discourse.

psychoanalysts to learn from the way literary critics, inspired by French theory in particular, have taken the liberty of subjecting classic psychoanalytic texts, Freud's in particular, to the same analytic scrutiny that psychoanalysts have reserved for their clinical cases (see, for example, Irigaray 1985; Bernheimer & Kahane 1985). This method of returning to and rereading original texts treats a theory not as an indissoluble whole but rather as a site of different, sometimes contradictory, vectors that need not or cannot be resolved into consistency (as psychoanalysts, including Lacan, long persisted in treating Freud: "he really means this"). The appearance of consistency was won only at the price of excluding or repressing what would disrupt its unity; now, instead, hints of this alterity are deliberately sought in the text.

Equally important, critical theory and poststructural thought have questioned the objective standpoint of knowledge as absolute and privileged, in favor of recognizing the "subject position" from which that theory is developed (Foucault 1972; see Fuss 1989). This perspectivism "decenters" theory and would be an especially pertinent criticism of some of the framing of arguments in psychoanalytic circles. To decenter theory is to move away from explanatory positions that postulate one central hub, one motivating principle (or two conflicting, interlocking ones), propelling one dynamic system, which thus can be seamlessly explained. It means reflecting on the perspective of our knowledge and accepting the paradoxes that can arise from an ability to identify with more than one perspective. To accept paradox is to contain rather than resolve contradictions, to sustain tension between elements heretofore defined as antithetical.

More difficult to integrate in psychoanalysis is the postmodern feminist attack on essentialist positions, especially the notion of identity. This feminist stance is often derived from

Foucault (see Butler 1990), who contended that identities are not derived from essences but constructed by discourse. This position requires us to delineate the way in which discursive systems of knowledge actually "produce" the categories by which we recognize ourselves to *be* the containers of such identities. Here the point is not only to reject the biological, transhistorical foundations of sexuality and gender — even to deconstruct the very category of "nature" — which rationalized masculine claims to power in traditional thought. It is also to rebut all claims from the feminist side, which might deploy and defend a naturalized female identity; to critique not only any natural foundation of Man's prerogatives but also the notion of "Woman." Thus it has been said that Woman is a "name" (Riley 1988) that makes woman appear to be the same kind of unitary subject as was the male subject of philosophical and political discourse and that works to suppress all other differences (race, class, sexual choice; see Scott 1988). It uses the frame of gender to create a false identity.

In this perspective, to locate individual or groups of women within the terms of the binary opposition men-women is as likely to be constricting as liberating. However, even though the original feminist emphasis on the singular sexual opposition man-woman may have obscured many other differences, it opened up a necessary intellectual space (de Lauretis 1994) in which the real social and psychological effects of that opposition on our world could be observed. I think it just as necessary to keep widening that space — one that we usually refer to with the category gender — as to create multidimensionality by putting its plane in intersection with other categorical spaces. In other words, we may recognize that "Woman" is not a unitary identity, and we may continually test the frame of gender. Proceeding deconstructively, we recognize that gender is both reified and elusive, rigid and porous, organizing and self-contradictory (Harris

1991; Dimen 1991). As Goldner (1991) has stated, we may accept gender as a paradoxical condition of our theory, "a transcendent analytic category whose truth, though false, remains central to thought; indeed, it constructs the very analytic categories we would use to deconstruct it" (p. 256). If we need to proliferate our questions through other frames, still we cannot simply dispense with the frame of binary gender opposition, especially in psychoanalysis. In the psychic world, where such binary oppositions play a major role in organizing our experience, that frame reveals many conflicts and provides a background for many other differences. And, of course, gender oppositions are so central to the history of psychoanalysis as a discourse that even when they figure as obstacles and omissions we are continually required to return to them.

A further problem that arises when we try to incorporate feminist theory into current psychoanalytic thought is whether the philosophical and critical discussions of "the subject" in feminist theory can properly be transferred to psychoanalysis. Despite my affinity for the decentering stance of contemporary feminist theory in general and the effort to deconstruct the notion of an essential female identity in particular, the sometimes radical rejection of subjectivity and the denial of what we might call the generalizable features of the psyche appear to me deeply incompatible with psychoanalysis (Benjamin 1994). The rejection by postmodern feminist theory of any unitary subject or self on the grounds that it is essentialist (Butler 1990; Fuss 1989; see Flax 1990) seems to present as many difficulties as it resolves. In particular, it seems to confuse the category of the epistemological, thinking subject with that of the self as a locus of subjective experience, unconscious as well as conscious, when, in fact, these operate on very different registers.[3] The

3. A more complicated issue, which I address elsewhere (Benjamin 1994), is that the theoretical underpinning of this position is the Lacanian idea that the subject is "split" (Rose 1982), which is specifically adumbrated at the level of

term *subject* as it is used in psychoanalysis refers to such a locus of experience, one that need not be centrally organized, coherent, or unified. Yet it can still allow continuity and awareness of different states of mind, can still feel more or less real or alive, can be more or less capable of recognizing or feeling the impact of the other. While it seems that psychoanalysts might benefit from accepting the challenge to modernist ideas of subjectivity posed by the deconstructionist formulations of Derrida (1976, 1978, 1982; see Culler 1982) or by the poststructuralist position of Foucault (1972, 1980), there may still be deep incompatibilities between the philosophical critique of the subject and current psychoanalytic thought.

Psychoanalysis has to retain some notion of the subject as a self, a historical being that preserves its history in the unconscious, whatever skepticism we allow about reaching the truth of that history. Even if the self is not unitary but has multiple positions and voices, psychoanalysis must be able to conceive of the person's singularity, his or her aesthetic or unique idiom (Bollas 1992). Even if the subject's positions are "constructed," psychoanalysis must imagine someone who does or does not own them (Rivera 1989). And precisely because psychoanalysis claims that something else that is not-I (not ego but *It*) speaks, that the self is split and the unconsciousness is unknown, It must also be considered to belong to the self. And this idea of an otherness within, an unconscious, unavoidably both transforms and preserves (*Aufhebung*) the idea of a transhistorical, essential self: not a Cartesian ego, not even all ego, but still a being separately embodied, and in that sense an individual psyche.

It is nonetheless important to ask how the critique of a

psychoanalysis but may still be seen as largely determined by Lacan's philosophical project of attacking the Cartesian ego. It tends to draw strength by polemicizing against a unitary ego that has, in fact, few living defenders, as if it had not been dispatched by earlier modernist criticism (Whitebook 1994).

transhistorical subject or of identity posed from a philosophical standpoint might be relevant to the concept of self that emerges from the phenomenal world of the psyche that we address in psychoanalysis. In fact, relational psychoanalysis has arrived at its own form of this questioning of the subject as absolute. The challenge to the assumption of a unitary subject is currently vital to psychoanalysts concerned with the two-person view. One aspect of that challenge has been formulated in terms that question whether any aspect of subjectivity can be privileged as the central, deeper, or truer part in relation to which other parts are epiphenomenal, superficial, inauthentic (S. Mitchell 1993; Bromberg 1993).

Another aspect of the challenge to the subject's encapsulated identity derives from an appreciation of the emotional transmission that occurs between any two subjects (Spezzano 1993), indeed, of the primacy of affective exchange early in life (D. Stern 1985). It also derives from a clinical experience that sees the analytic exchange as the expression not merely of an internal conflict between repression and unconscious wishes, defense, and drives but of the active search to find emotional resonance in the other—perhaps to evacuate mental contents or perhaps to represent and share feelings that cannot be borne alone (Sandler 1992; Spezzano 1994). This relational perspective makes the analyst's countertransference central not merely as a source of information but as unconscious communication that demonstrates the effect the patient can have, an effect that the analyst must process and return to the patient in more usable form. It makes of the analyst's interpretation a relational event (S. Mitchell 1988). The constructivist (D. B. Stern 1992; Hoffman 1983, 1991, 1994) or perspectivist (Aron 1992) view explicitly expands the emphasis on countertransference as effect to ask how the two-person analytic relationship affects what is known and interpreted rather than merely constituting a context in which the patient's subjectivity is discovered as an already existing thing. As Aron (1992) suggests, the mutuality of influence between analyst and analysand can be recognized while preserving asymmetry of roles. The tension between mutuality and asymmetry can be productive, as Hoffman (1994) shows: against the backdrop of idealization of the analyst's role, the experience of mutuality may be especially meaningful. The analyst, aware of using his or her subjectivity, incorporates the elements of uncertainty and difference (Bollas 1989) within the expression of the interpretation, as if to say, "This may be true of you, or merely of you with me, or merely my perception of you based on my own experience. I may not always think this to be true. You or I may disagree." At this point of indeterminacy, a meeting of psychoanalysis with contemporary theory could be instructive to both.

Sadly, postmodern feminist theory and North American psychoanalysis have assimilated few of one another's contributions. Having adopted Lacan, whose critique of ego psychology more than forty years ago pointed to the problems of assuming a unitary, cohesive self, postmodern feminists have applied that critique to object relations theory. In so doing, they have framed Lacanian theory and object relations theory as antithetical positions and have shown little interest in developing a discussion between them. One aim of the essays that follow is to suggest some of the points around which a fruitful dispute — a confrontation with difference — might develop. Another is to delineate those dilemmas of gender that can be understood by reference to the issues of envy and loss, identification and repudiation, that object relations theory has foregrounded. This may serve to clarify the different perspective that emerges from such issues in contrast to the appeal to a central principle of sexual difference (having or reflecting the phallus), as Lacan posits. It may turn out that this relational perspective has a heretofore unobserved congruence with contemporary feminist thought. Ironically, to posit a central complex as organizer of difference seems to be at odds with the decentering aims of the postmodern critique.

For I hope to show that, dispensing with its totalizing aspects, the feminist critique of identity can be assimilated by a relational perspective to stimulate a deeper consideration of the multiplicity and ambiguity of gender identifications (see Chapters 2, 4, and 5). Indeed, while some proponents of the Lacanian position assume that the self must be constructed through its gender position and therefore that the instability of gender boundaries must be associated with psychotic confusion or anxiety (see Baruch and Serrano 1987), the relational perspective offers another way to think about divisions in the self (Dimen 1991). It is more likely to accept the ambiguity and multiplicity of cross-sex identifications from the preoedipal phase, to embrace the truth of gender incoherence against the "false self" appearance of gender stability (Goldner 1991). Nor does it require—as some critics have claimed—the assumption that identifications produce a unitary gender identity. Rather, it suggests the idea of recuperating through symbolic representations the multiplicity of the overinclusive phase (Bassin 1994) and preserving that phase, with its grandiose aspirations, alongside the oedipal and postoedipal differentiation of gender (Aron 1995). This recuperation of multiplicity fits with recent theorizing by relational analysts of multiple self-states (Bromberg 1993; Rivera 1989) that may be more or less linked in different individuals. Such notions parallel many of the arguments made by feminist theorists about preserving the multiple positions of the *I* (Fuss 1989; Benjamin 1994).

To illustrate the complexity of identification, I show how identifications work to allow the integration of difference, preserving rather than assimilating different self-positions. Thus girls do not achieve a coherent femininity simply through un-broken identification with their mothers but rather preserve the early longing for identification with their fathers — if only nega-tively, in the form of ideal love of masculinity (Chapter 4).[4] Likewise, I have questioned the idea that boys need simply to disidentify with mother (Greenson 1968), and argued that such disowned identifications with mother reappear in feelings of loss and envy (Chapter 3). To articulate this idea more sharply, women's and men's identifications are always multiple, and the upshot of relinquishing crucial "identifications with differ-ence" is that difference is defensively incorporated into rigid representations rather than recognized in tension with com-monality.

In *The Bonds of Love* I suggested that the recognition of difference is more likely to be blocked by the splitting of gender in the exclusive heterosexual complementarity of the oedipal position than by the overinclusive identifications of the pre-oedipal. But I did not draw from this the obvious critique of the psychoanalytic theory of homosexuality as a "failure" of hetero-sexuality. Having become mindful of this omission, thanks to the many criticisms of my work on this point (see especially O'Connor & Ryan 1993), I have also become more sensitive to the way that psychoanalysts by and large continue to idealize heterosexual development uncritically and to pathologize homosexuality (see Chodorow 1994). It is noteworthy that psy-choanalysis has ignored the by now commonplace critique of such normative stances and their implication in stigmatization

4. My emphasis on raising to consciousness the identificatory love of the pre-oedipal father is sometimes understood as diminishing the importance of the girl's feminine, oedipal love. But in this case, as elsewhere, my intention is only to il-luminate the less-explored territory, not to obscure the familiar. As I reiterate, there is no need for either/or regarding oedipal and preoedipal, genital and pregenital loves. This both/and applies to the erotic transference as well (see Lachmann 1994).

and social control. The need to hold onto a regulatory ideal of heterosexuality surely has many historical and current sources, not the least of which is the legitimation of psychoanalysis as a profession.

In any event, several essays in this book elaborate the implications of the idea that multiple identifications are formative for all sexual relations and that object choice and identification are not the simple inverse of each other. In suggesting that identification and object love do not break down along the clear lines suggested by the oedipal model, that identificatory love may be — perhaps should be — the basis of object love, I question the superficial distinction made between heterosexual and homosexual choice. What appears consciously to be hetero or homo may not be so in unconscious fantasy: whether one seeks likeness or difference is not determined simply by the nominal gender of one's partner (Harris 1991). Nor do others appear to us simply as like or different; rather, they appear in complex combinations that reflect the multiplicity of our and their gendered positions.

A further issue to be considered is that the oedipal structure of heterosexual complementarity, uncritically promulgated in psychoanalysis, entails deep sacrifice — sacrifice that the oedipal principle of mutual exclusivity serves to naturalize and conceal. As I first proposed in my discussion of erotic domination (Benjamin 1980) and elaborated in *The Bonds of Love*, the complementary relationship works through splitting: the subject now fills the position of the other (sex) not with an outside, differentiated being but with the self's disowned, unconscious experience, which appears as a threatening Other. The historical relation of women's subordination to men can be analyzed as the paradigmatic expression of splitting: the subject simultaneously denies the other's subjectivity and makes her, instead, into the object that embodies the split-off parts of self.

In my discussion of the fantasy of the omnipotent mother (Chapter 3) I show how the twin acts of denying maternal subjectivity and repudiating identification underlie men's dread of the mother, whether the dread is expressed as denigration or idealization of her as other. But I also suggest that what counters the apparition of the split-off other — the symbolic space of early maternal intersubjective relatedness — may be recuperated without creating a countermyth of a "harmonious" maternal ideal (Scott 1993). As I showed in *The Bonds of Love*, viewing the earliest experience of the mother from her perspective breaks up this myth, confronting her with the paradoxical necessity of recognizing, while not yet "knowing," the strange newborn who was once part of her body. Indeed, the struggle for recognition inevitably breaks up the ideal, expresses and brings forth aggression and separation, and so helps foster a symbolic space within the early maternal dyad between mother and child — a process previously conceptualized exclusively in terms of the oedipal father-son rivalry.

This revised notion of an earlier symbolic space is crucial to conceptualizing the intersubjective aspects of both the analytic dyad and the maternal relationship. In my discussion of pornography (Chapter 6) I continue to explore the tension between the intersubjective acknowledgment of the other and the intrapsychic relation to the fantasy object, derogated or ideal. The outcome of fantasy — of the dualities of sex and aggression, "heaven or hell" — is, I think, different according to whether the symbolic space of intersubjectivity is retained or closed. In my discussion of the erotic transference (Chapter 5) I emphasize this symbolic space as we experience it in the psychoanalytic situation. I consider some ways in which we might contrast the intersubjective experience of being alone yet together in the analytic space with the experience of idealizing, identificatory love of the analyst. While I show how these different takes on the analytic experience are imbricated with the gendered representations of maternal holding and phallic knowing, my intention is not to make these gender metaphors formulaic. As in my discussion of the appearance of the daughter's paternal identification in the transference (Chapter 4), I want to base the uses of gender constructs not on a naturalized notion of their origins but on a sense of their contradictory appearance in culturally pervasive, unconsciously rooted, and consciously stereotyped maternal and paternal ideals.

While I often emphasize raising to the surface of our knowledge the less explicated side of intersubjectivity, I am equally concerned that idealization/identification be articulated and examined for its positive as well as its negative valence. The matter to which I return again and again, in different ways, is the tension between intersubjectivity and the dimension of the intrapsychic that I call the *Ideal*. Like many such bifurcations, I suspect that this division inevitably leads to contradictions and irresolution. The very word *Ideal* has more than one valence, referring both to idealization and to ideals or goals. But a particular ambiguity arises because the notion of the intersubjective may not only stand in contrast to idealized experience; intersubjectivity itself may be taken as a normative ideal — indeed, may be uncritically assumed to be such an ideal. Here the distinction between a philosophical and a psychoanalytic register may be of some use. A recent philosophical critique of my work (Meehan 1994) suggests that my account of the infant's development of intersubjectivity conflates the normative ideal of mutual recognition with the empirical possibility and necessity of development. "The assumption that to recognize the other is a social need or a normative ideal in no way entails the assumption that we are born with the ability to do so" (Weir 1992, quoted in Meehan 1994). My argument does not begin with a normative ideal but with a material possibility. The point I hoped I was making was not that human beings necessarily develop this ability but that we can presume some innate capacities for such development — capacities for which Daniel Stern (1985) has made a strong empirical case — and that these capacities had long been excluded from the Freudian view of the baby. Thus mutual recognition derives from material possibility, but whether it will be realized and in what way are in no sense predetermined. The idea is not to bolster the ideal by proving that we are "born with the ability"; it is to recognize that when we postulate a psychological *need* (not a social need or a normative ideal) for recognition, we mean that failure to satisfy the need will inevitably result in difficulties or even damage to the psyche.

Whether normative ideals should be extrapolated from such postulates is another matter. Here the problem of what it means to have an ideal becomes complicated, depending on whether we are speaking in the psychoanalytic or the philosophical register. This tension between the two views remains a source of difficulty, and my way of handling it in *The Bonds of Love* is certainly open to question. On the one hand, I stated that we need mutual recognition in order to develop our faculties, a statement that postulates a kind of essential, developmental position that is typical of psychoanalysis; on the other hand, I argued from the standpoint of social and political theory that we need mutual recognition in order to live in some degree free of domination and nonviolently. I linked these two positions by arguing that the upshot of failures of recognition is domination, that the constitution of subjectivity and the self-other relationship is a necessary material basis for noncoercive intersubjectivity (Meehan 1994). Habermas has put forth this kind of intersubjectivity as a normative ideal, but my goals were more modest. I wished to remain within the theoretical space long assumed by psychoanalysis, in which such arguments could be made without taking up directly the meaning of recognition as a philosophical ideal. To satisfy such philosophical criteria would constitute a far broader task, which others may better undertake (see Honneth 1993).

I meant to confine my remarks primarily to recognition as a psychoanalytic category, to postulate a dimension of psychic capability, to offer a standpoint from which we could analyze the self-other relation, and to keep that relation in tandem with the intrapsychic categories of Freudian thought. Nor was it my intent to replace Habermas's idea of autonomy with mutual recognition (Meehan 1994) as a category that forms the basis for intersubjectivity, which implies an opposition between autonomy and recognition.[5] In my thinking, the concept of mutual recognition includes autonomy — or, rather, preserves and transforms it as a pole of the necessary tension of independence/dependence between subjects, of differentiation. To oppose the idea of recognition to that of autonomy would be misleading or self-contradictory, for it would deny the fact that recognition requires acceptance of the other's independence and unknowability (Cornell 1992). This limit to knowledge is a crucial condition of individuation, for, as Bollas says, "to know the other and to be known is as much an act of unconscious evocation that parts the subjects and announces the solitude of the self" (1992) as it is an act of comprehension.

Further, the concept of mutual recognition should include the notion of breakdown, of failure to sustain that tension, as well as account for the possibility of repair after failure (see Chapter 1). In this framework, the attunement within the

5. Meehan's (1994) critique assumes that I throw out not only autonomy but also rationality because I adopt Horkheimer and Adorno's critique of rationality in *Dialectic of Enlightenment.* In any event, I stated clearly that I had in mind Keller's (1985) concept of dynamic objectivity, that the "feminist critique of rationality leads us to redraft our map of the mind to include the territory of self and other. . . . [It] is not a proposal to scrap [rationality] in favor of romantic antirationality . . . [but one to] redefine rationality and expand its boundaries."

mother-infant relationship is not to be conflated with a normative ideal of mutuality. Nor is attunement itself equatable with
full recognition of the other; rather, it is only one of the earliest
forms in which knowing the other is found, part of a long development of the capacity for recognition. Thus the relationship itself is not meant to be idealized, seen as some kind of
should-be harmony, to which we hope to return; its forms of
connection may be oppressive or facilitating, controlling or liberating.[6] Examining the early struggle for recognition — which
includes failure, destruction, aggression, even when it is working — ought to show us something about our relation to ideals:
mutual recognition is meaningful as an ideal only when it is
understood as the basis for struggle and negotiation of conflict
(see Pizer 1992), when its impossibility and the striving to attain
it are adequately included in the concept (see Butler 1994).

This necessity of grasping the negative moment is something that I have tried to emphasize more clearly in these essays.
However, the basic formal logic of my argument remains essentially the same as in my earlier work: reintegrating the excluded,
negative moment to create a sustained tension rather than an
opposition. This logic holds whether we are talking about the
relation between self and other that the ideal of masculine rationality and autonomy have excluded or about the necessity of

6. This misunderstanding, for which I am perhaps responsible, is manifest by
those who argue against me from the poststructural-deconstructionist side (Scott
1993) that eschews normativity, as well as those who argue from the Habermasian
defense of normativity. In the latter case, for instance, Benhabib (1995) tends to
see my work as a defense of a balance between autonomy and connection without
noticing my point that this balance necessarily breaks down and opens the field to
domination — indeed, that these two ideals cannot be simply set up as happy complements. Meehan, on the other hand, thinks that I throw out autonomy. In fact,
my effort is to set up a more complex relation among all of these terms that
"holds" the continual struggle to recognize an other — a struggle with multiple
and perhaps, finally, obscure origins, with many difficulties and impediments —
without losing sight of the ideal possibility that sometimes mutual recognition and
respect for difference can be realized.

destruction that the ideal of recognition might exclude. But whereas this logic replicates certain moves elaborated in deconstruction — reversing and elevating the negated element in an opposition — the practice of psychoanalysis pushes toward something rather different. The lost possibilities of theory have to lead us toward a reconstruction of what we encounter in practice. As a psychoanalyst, it is not enough to say that destruction is recognition's other side: we have to know it when we see it at work, to know why we sometimes fail to grasp it; at least we have to try.

To postulate an intersubjective dimension of recognition is not merely to think about something that has been left out, excluded, put on the margin of psychoanalysis. Nor is it constituted as a necessary opposite to the intrapsychic. If we were to think of intersubjective theory primarily as something left out or unframed by intrapsychic theory, that would be to leave it in the position of an abstraction (an abstract negation) rather than to open it up as a concrete site of discovery and exploration. In fact, that site has become central to thinking about the analytic endeavor, in leading to a practical focus on the countertransference, the analyst's subjectivity, and the unknowability or knowability of the patient's subjectivity — in short, the intense scrutiny of the meeting of two minds, each with a multiplicity of its own.

In the past several years psychoanalytic work has undergone a radical change. The manifold ways in which we now try to grasp the meaning of the unconscious in terms of communication between ourselves and the other subject in the room have opened up the dialogic possibilities of intersubjectivity. The unknowability and uncertainty that we consciously acknowledge, our sense of the multiple possibilities of interpretation in any moment (as well as of the limits of our knowledge), our realization of the likelihood that we will communicate our subjectivity whether we wish to or not, the possibility of speaking from our own responses and doubts within the analytic situation — all of these give a greater practical scope to the question of recognition than was previously imagined. To speak of recognition is thus to speak as much out of our sense of limit as out of our desire, and to find a way to poise ourselves between the two.

The evolution of our questioning necessarily brings about a more complex experience within the psychoanalytic situation itself. And then again, as this complicated force field emerges in our practice, we seek a way to represent it theoretically. I see these essays as part of that wider search to represent and articulate experience in a space that always existed in psychoanalysis but was previously unformulated. In turn, such articulation allows more of that experience to find its way into our consciousness, that otherness by which we are always likely to be surprised.

1 / Recognition and Destruction:
An Outline of Intersubjectivity

We are all of us born in moral stupidity, taking the world as an udder to feed our supreme selves: Dorothea had early begun to emerge from that stupidity, but yet it had been easier for her to imagine how she would . . . become wise and strong in his strength and wisdom, than to conceive with that distinctness which is no longer reflection but feeling . . . that he had an equivalent center of self, whence the lights and shadows must always fall with a certain difference.
George Eliot, *Middlemarch*

In recent years analysts from diverse psychoanalytic schools have converged in the effort to formulate relational theories of the self (Eagle 1984, S. Mitchell 1988). What these approaches share is the belief that the human mind is interactive rather than monadic, that the psychoanalytic process should be understood as occurring between subjects rather than within the individual

An earlier version of this essay appeared as "An Outline of Intersubjectivity: The Development of Recognition" in *Psychoanalytic Psychology* 7 (1990), Supplement, 33–46, and in N. Skolnick and S. Warshaw, *Relational Perspectives in Psychoanalysis* (Hillsdale, N.J.: Analytic Press, 1993). Used by permission.

(Atwood and Stolorow 1984, S. Mitchell 1988). Mental life is seen from an intersubjective perspective. Although this perspective has transformed both our theory and our practice in important ways, such transformations create new problems. A theory in which the individual subject no longer reigns absolute must confront the difficulty each subject has in recognizing the other as an equivalent center of experience (Benjamin 1988).

The problem of recognizing the other emerges the moment we consider that troublesome legacy of intrapsychic theory, the term *object*. In the original usage, still common in self psychology and object relations theories, the concept of object relations refers to the psychic internalization and representation of interactions between self and objects. While such theories ascribe a considerable role to the early environment and parental objects—in short, "real" others—they have taken us only to the point of recognizing that "where ego is, objects must be." So, for example, neither Fairbairn's insistence on the need for the whole object nor Kohut's declaration that selfobjects remain important throughout life addresses directly the difference between object and other. Perhaps the elision between "real" others and their internal representation is so widely tolerated because the epistemological question of what is reality and what is representation appears to us—in our justifiable humility—too ecumenical and lofty for our parochial craft. Or perhaps, as psychoanalysts, we are not really troubled by the question of reality.

But the unfortunate tendency to collapse other subjects into the rubric *objects* cannot be ascribed simply to this irresoluteness regarding reality. Nor can it be dismissed as a terminological embarrassment that greater linguistic precision might dissolve (see Kohut 1984). Rather, it is a symptom of the very problems in psychoanalysis that a relational theory should aim to cure. The inquiry into the intersubjective dimension of the analytic encounter would aim to change our theory and practice so that "where objects were, subjects must be."

What does such a change mean? A beginning has been made with the introduction of the term *intersubjectivity* — the field of intersection between two subjectivities, the interplay between two different subjective worlds to define the analytic situation (Atwood and Stolorow 1984; Stolorow, Brandschaft, and Atwood 1987). But how is the meeting of two subjects different from the meeting of a subject and an object? Once we have acknowledged that the object makes an important contribution to the life of the subject, what is added by deciding to call this object another subject? And what are the impediments to the meeting of two minds?

To begin this inquiry, we must ask: what difference does the other make, the other who is truly perceived as outside, distinct from our mental field of operations? Isn't there a dramatic difference between the experience with the other perceived as outside the self and that with the subjectively conceived object? Winnicott formulated the basic outlines of this distinction in what may well be considered his most daring and radical statement, "The Use of an Object and Relating Through Identifications" (1969b). Since then, with a few recent exceptions (Eigen 1981, Modell 1984, Ghent 1989, Bollas 1989), there has been little effort to elaborate Winnicott's juxtaposition of the two possible relationships to the object. Yet, as I will show, the difference between the other as subject and the other as object is crucial for a relational psychoanalysis.

The distinction between the two types of relationships to the other can emerge clearly only if we acknowledge that both are endemic to psychic experience and hence are valid areas of psychoanalytic knowledge. If there is a contradiction between the two modes of experience, then we ought to probe it as a condition of knowledge rather than assume it to be a fork in the road. Other theoretical grids that have split psychoanalytic thought — drive theory versus object relations theory, ego versus id psychology, intrapsychic versus interpersonal theory — insisted on a choice between opposing perspectives. I am proposing, instead, that the two dimensions of experience with the object/other are complementary, though they sometimes stand in an oppositional relationship. By embracing both dimensions, we can fulfill the intention of relational theories: to account both for the pervasive effects of human relationships on psychic development and for the equally ubiquitous effects of internal psychic mechanisms and fantasies in shaping psychological life and interaction.

I refer to the two categories of experience as the intrapsychic and the intersubjective dimensions (Benjamin 1988). The idea of intersubjectivity, which has been brought into psychoanalysis from philosophy (Habermas 1970, 1971, 1992), is useful because it specifically addresses the problem of defining the other as object. Intersubjectivity was formulated in deliberate contrast to the logic of subject and object, which predominates in Western philosophy and science. It refers to that zone of experience or theory in which the other is not merely the object of the ego's need/drive or cognition/perception but has a separate and equivalent center of self.

Intersubjective theory postulates that the other must be recognized as another subject in order for the self to fully experience his or her subjectivity in the other's presence. This means that we have a need for recognition and that we have a capacity to recognize others in return, thus making mutual recognition possible. But recognition is a capacity of individual development that is only unevenly realized — in a sense, the point of a relational psychoanalysis is to explain this fact. In Freudian metapsychology the process of recognizing the other "with that distinctness which is no longer reflection but feeling" would appear, at best, as a background effect of the relationship between ego and external reality. Feminist critics of psychoanalysis have suggested that the conceptualization of the first other, the mother, as an object underlies this theoretical lacuna. The cultural antithesis between male subject and female object contributed much to the failure to take into account the subjectivity of the other. Denial of the mother's subjectivity, in theory and in practice, profoundly impedes our ability to see the world as inhabited by equal subjects. My purpose is to show that, in fact, the capacity to recognize the mother as a subject is an important part of early development, and to bring the process of recognition into the foreground of our thinking.

I will suggest some preliminary outlines of the development of the capacity for recognition. In particular, I will focus on separation-individuation theory, showing how much more it can reveal when it is viewed through the intersubjective lens, especially in light of the contributions of both Daniel Stern and Winnicott. Because separation-individuation theory is formulated in terms of ego and object, it does not fully realize its own potential contribution. In the ego-object perspective the child is the individual, is seen as moving in a progression toward autonomy and separateness. The telos of this process is the creation of psychic structure through internalization of the object in the service of greater independence. Separation-individuation theory thus focuses on the structural residue of the child's interaction with the mother as object; it leaves in the unexamined background the aspects of engagement, connection, and active assertion that occur with the mother as other. This perspective is infantocentric, unconcerned with the source of the mother's responses, which reflect not only her pathology or health ("narcissistic" versus "good enough") but also her necessarily independent subjectivity. It also misses the *pleasure* of the evolving relationship with a partner from whom one knows how to elicit a response but whose responses are not entirely predictable and assimilable to internal fantasy. The idea of pleasure was lost when ego psychology put the id on the back burner, but it might be restored by recognizing the subjectivity of the other.

An intersubjective perspective helps us transcend the infantocentric viewpoint of intrapsychic theory by asking how a person becomes capable of enjoying recognition with an other. Logically, recognizing the parent as subject cannot be the result simply of internalizing her as mental object. This is a developmental process that has barely begun to be explicated. How does a child develop into a person who, as a parent, is able to recognize her or his own child? What are the internal processes, the psychic landmarks, of such development? Where is the theory that tracks the development of the child's responsiveness, empathy, and concern, and not just the parent's sufficiency or failure?

It is in regard to these questions that most theories of the self have fallen short. Even self psychology, which has placed such emphasis on attunement and empathy and has focused on the intersubjectivity of the analytic encounter, has been tacitly one-sided in its understanding of the parent-child relationship and the development of intersubjective relatedness. Perhaps in reaction against the oedipal reality principle, Kohut (1977, 1984) defined the necessary confrontation with the other's needs or with limits in a self-referential way — optimal failures in empathy (parallel to analysts' errors) — as if there were nothing for children to learn about the other's rights or feelings. Although Kohut's goal was to enable individuals to open "new channels of empathy" and "in-tuneness between self and selfobject" (1984, p. 66), the self was always the recipient, not the giver, of empathy. The responsiveness of the selfobject by definition serves the function of "shoring up our self" throughout life; but at what point are we concerned with the responsiveness of the outside other whom we love? The occasionally mentioned (perhaps more frequently assumed) "love object," who would presumably hold the place of outside other, has no articulated place in the theory. Thus, once again, the pleasure in mutuality between two subjects is reduced to its function of stabilizing the self, not of enlarging our awareness of the outside or of recognizing others as animated by independent, though similar, feelings.[1]

In this essay I would like to outline some crucial points in the development of recognition. It is certainly true that recognition begins with the other's confirming response, which tells us that we have created meaning, had an impact, revealed an intention. But very early on we find that recognition between persons—understanding and being understood, being in attunement—is becoming an end in itself. Recognition between persons is essentially mutual. By our very enjoyment of the other's confirming response, we recognize her in return. What the research on mother-infant interaction has uncovered about early reciprocity and mutual influence is best conceptualized as the development of the capacity for mutual recognition. The frame-by-frame studies of face-to-face play at three or four months of age have given us a kind of early history of recognition.

The pathbreaking work of Stern (1974, 1977, 1985) and the more recent contributions of Beebe (Beebe and Stern 1977, Beebe 1985, Beebe and Lachmann 1988) have illuminated how crucial the relationship of mutual influence is for early self-development. They have also shown that self-regulation is

1. My remarks are more apt for Kohut and early self psychology. Later writings show some tendency to correct this one-sidedness, to include the evolution of difference (e.g., Lachmann 1986) and the relationship to the object as other (Stolorow 1986).

achieved at this point through regulating the other: I can change my own mental state by causing the other to be more or less stimulating. Mother's recognition is the basis for the baby's sense of agency. Equally important, although less emphasized, is the other side of this play interaction: the mother is dependent to some degree on the baby's recognition. A baby who is less responsive is a less "recognizing" baby, and the mother who reacts to her apathetic or fussy baby by overstimulating or withdrawing is a mother feeling despair that the baby does not recognize her.

In Stern's view, however, early play does not yet constitute intersubjective relatedness (1985). Rather, he designates the next phase, when affective attunement develops at eight or nine months of age, as intersubjectivity proper. This is the moment when we discover that "there are other minds out there!" and that separate minds can share a similar state. I would agree that this phase constitutes an advance in recognition of the other, but the earlier interaction can be considered an antecedent in the form of concrete affective sharing. Certainly, from the standpoint of the mother whose infant returns her smile this is already the beginning of reciprocal recognition. Therefore, rather than designate the later phase as intersubjective relatedness, I would conceptualize a development of intersubjectivity in which there are key moments of transformation.

In this phase, as Stern (1985) emphasizes, the new thing is the sharing of the inner world. The infant begins to check out how the parent feels when the infant is discovering a new toy, and the parent demonstrates attunement by responding in another medium. By translating the same affective level into another modality — for example, from kinetic to vocal — the adult conveys the crucial fact that it is the *inner* experience that is congruent. The difference in form makes the element of similarity or sharing clear. I would add, the parent is not literally sharing the same state, for the parent is (usually) excited by the infant's reaction, not by the toy itself. The parent is in fact taking pleasure in *contacting the child's mind.*

This is a good point at which to consider the contrast between intersubjective theory and ego psychology, a contrast that Stern stresses. The phase of discovering other minds coincides roughly with Mahler's differentiation and practicing, but there is an important difference in emphasis. In the intersubjective view, the infant's greater separation, which Mahler underscores in this period, actually proceeds in tandem with and enhances the felt connection with the other. The joy of intersubjective attunement is: This *Other* can share my feeling. According to Mahler (Mahler, Pine, and Bergmann 1975), though, the infant of ten months is primarily involved in exploring, in the "love affair with the world." The checking back to look at mother is not about sharing the experience but about safety/anxiety issues, "refueling." This is a phase in which Mahler sees the mother not as contacting the child's mind but as giving him or her a push from the nest.

While Stern emphasizes his differences with Mahler, I think the two models are complementary, not mutually exclusive. It seems to me that intersubjective theory amplifies separation-individuation theory at this point by focusing on the affective exchange between parent and child and by stressing the simultaneity of connection and separation. Instead of opposite endpoints of a longitudinal trajectory, connection and separation form a tension that requires the equal magnetism of both sides.

It is this tension between connection and separation that I want to track beyond the period of affective attunement. If we follow it into the second year of life, we can see a tension developing between assertion of self and recognition of the other. Translating Mahler's rapprochement crisis into the terms of intersubjectivity, we can say that in this crisis the tension between asserting self and recognizing the other breaks down and is manifested as a conflict between self and other.

My analysis of this crisis derives, in part, from philosophy, from Hegel's formulation of the problem of recognition in *The Phenomenology of Spirit*. In his discussion of the conflict between "the independence and dependence of self-consciousness" Hegel showed how the self's wish for absolute independence conflicts with the self's need for recognition. In trying to establish itself as an independent entity, the self must yet recognize the other as a subject like itself in order to be recognized by the other. This immediately compromises the self's absoluteness and poses the problem that the other could be equally absolute and independent. Each self wants to be recognized and yet to maintain its absolute identity: the self says, I want to affect you, but I want nothing you do or say to affect me; I am who I am. In its encounter with the other, the self wishes to affirm its absolute independence, even though its need for the other and the other's similar wish undercut that affirmation.

This description of the self's absoluteness covers approximately the same territory as narcissism in Freudian theory, particularly its manifestation as omnipotence: the insistence on being one (everyone is identical to me) and all alone (there is nothing outside of me that I do not control). Freud's conception of the earliest ego (1911, 1915a), with its hostility to the outside or its incorporation of everything good into itself, is not unlike Hegel's absolute self. Hegel's notion of the conflict between independence and dependence meshes with the classic psychoanalytic view in which the self does not wish to give up omnipotence.

But even if we reject the Freudian view of the ego, the confrontation with the other's subjectivity and with the limits of self-assertion is difficult to negotiate. The need for recognition entails this fundamental paradox: at the very moment of realizing our own independent will, we are dependent upon another to recognize it. At the very moment we come to understand the meaning of I, *myself*, we are forced to see the limitations of that self. At the moment when we understand that separate minds can share similar feelings, we begin to learn that these minds can also disagree.

Let us return to Mahler's description of rapprochement and see how it illustrates the paradox of recognition and how the infant is supposed to negotiate that paradox. Before rapprochement, in the self-assertion of the practicing phase, the infant still takes herself for granted, and her mother as well. She does not make a sharp discrimination between doing things with mother's help and doing without it. She is too excited by *what* she is doing to reflect on *who* is doing it. Beginning when the child is about fourteen months of age, a conflict emerges between her grandiose aspirations and the perceived reality of her limitations and dependency. Although she is now able to do more, the toddler is aware of what she can't do and what she can't make mother do — for example, stay with her instead of going out. Many of the power struggles that begin here (wanting the whole pear, not a slice) can be summed up as a demand: "Recognize my intent!" She will insist that mother share everything, participate in all her deeds, acquiesce to all her demands. The toddler is also up against the increased awareness of separateness, and, consequently, of vulnerability: she can move away from mother — but mother can also move away from her.

If we reframe this description from the intersubjective perspective, the infant now knows that different minds can feel differently, that she is dependent as well as independent. In this sense, rapprochement is the crisis of recognizing the other — specifically, of confronting mother's independence. It is no accident that mother's leaving becomes a focal point here, for it confronts the child not only with separation but with the other's independent aims. For similar reasons, the mother may experience conflict at this point: the child's demands are now threatening, no longer simply needs but expressions of the child's independent (tyrannical) will. The child is different from the mother's own mental fantasy, no longer *her* object. The child may switch places with the mother, from passive to active. The omnipotence once attributed to the "good" all-giving mother now resides instead in the child. How the mother responds to her child's and her own aggression depends on her ability to mitigate such fantasies with a sense of real agency and separate selfhood, on her confidence in her child's ability to survive conflict, loss, imperfection. The mother has to be able both to set clear boundaries for her child and to recognize the child's will, both to insist on her own independence and to respect that of the child—in short, to balance assertion and recognition. If she cannot do this, omnipotence continues, attributed either to the mother or the self; in neither case can we say that the development of mutual recognition has been furthered.

From the standpoint of intersubjective theory, the ideal "resolution" of the paradox of recognition is that it continue as a *constant tension* between recognizing the other and asserting the self. In Mahler's theory, however, the rapprochement conflict appears to be resolved through internalization, the achievement of object constancy—when the child can separate from mother or be angry at her and still be able to contact her presence or goodness. In a sense, this resolution sets the goal of development too low: it is difficult and therefore sufficient for the child to accomplish the realistic integration of good and bad object representations (Kernberg 1980). The sparse formulation of the end of the rapprochement conflict is anticlimactic, leaving us to wonder, is this all? In this picture, the child has only to accept that mother can disappoint her; she does not begin to shift her center of gravity to recognize that mother does this because she has her own center.

The breakdown and re-creation of the tension between asserting one's own reality and accepting the other's is a neglected but equally important aspect of the crisis. This aspect emerges when we superimpose Winnicott's idea of destroying the object (1969b) on Mahler's rapprochement crisis. It is destruction — negation in Hegel's sense — that enables the subject to go beyond relating to the object through identification, projection, and other intrapsychic processes pertaining to the subjectively conceived object. Destruction makes possible the transition from relating (intrapsychic) to using the object, to carrying on a relationship with an other who is objectively perceived as existing outside the self, an entity in her own right. That is, in the mental act of negating or obliterating the object, which may be expressed in the real effort to attack the other, we find out whether the real other survives. If she survives without retaliating or withdrawing under the attack, then we know her to exist outside ourselves, not just as our mental product.

Winnicott's scheme can be expanded to postulate not a sequential relationship but rather a basic tension between denial and affirmation of the other, between omnipotence and recognition of reality. Another way to understand the conflicts that occur in rapprochement is through the concepts of destruction and survival: the wish to assert the self absolutely and deny everything outside one's own mental omnipotence must sometimes crash against the implacable reality of the other. In the collision Winnicott has in mind, however, aggression does not occur "reactive to the encounter with the reality principle" but rather "creates the quality of externality." When the destructiveness damages neither the parent nor the self, external reality comes into view as a sharp, distinct contrast to the inner fantasy world. The outcome of this process is not simply reparation or restoration of the good object (Eigen 1981; Ghent,1990) but love, the sense of discovering the other. ("I destroyed you!" "I love you!")

The flip side of Winnicott's analysis could be stated as follows: when destruction is not countered with survival, when the other's reality does not come into view, a defensive process of internalization takes place. Aggression becomes a problem — how to dispose of the bad feeling. ("What about waste-disposal?") What cannot be worked through and dissolved with the outside other is transposed into a drama of internal objects, shifting from the domain of the intersubjective into the domain of the intrapsychic. In real life, even when the other's response dissipates aggression, there is no perfect process of destruction and survival; there is always also internalization. All experience is elaborated intrapsychically, we might venture to say, but when the other does not survive and aggression is not dissipated, experience becomes almost exclusively intrapsychic. It therefore seems fallacious to regard internalization processes only as breakdown products or as defenses; rather, we could see them as a kind of underlying substratum of mental activity — a constant symbolic digestion process that constitutes an important part of the cycle of exchange between the individual and the outside. It is the loss of balance between the intrapsychic and the intersubjective, between fantasy and reality, that is the problem.

Indeed, the problem in psychoanalytic theory has been that internalization — either the defensive or the structure-building aspects, depending on which object relations theory you favor — has obscured the component of destruction that Winnicott emphasizes: discovering "that fantasy and fact, both important, are nevertheless different from each other" (1964, p. 62). The complementarity of the intrapsychic and intersubjective modalities is important here: as Winnicott makes clear, it is in contrast to the fantasy of destruction that the reality of survival is so satisfying and authentic.

Winnicott thus offers the notion of a reality that can be loved, something beyond the integration of good and bad. While the intrapsychic ego has reality imposed from without, the intersubjective ego discovers reality. This reality principle does not represent a detour to wish fulfillment or a modification of the pleasure principle. Nor is it the acceptance of a false life of adaptation. Rather, it is a continuation under more complex conditions of the infant's original fascination with and love of what is outside, her appreciation of difference and novelty. This appreciation is the element in differentiation that gives separation its positive, rather than simply hostile, coloring: love of the world, not merely leaving or distancing from mother. To the extent that mother herself is placed outside, she can be loved; then separation is truly the other side of connection to the other.

It is this appreciation of the other's reality that completes the picture of separation and explains what there is beyond internalization: the establishment of shared reality. Elsa First (1988) has provided some relevant observations of how the toddler begins to apprehend mutuality as a concomitant of separateness — specifically, in relation to the mother's leaving. The vehicle of this resolution is, expanding Winnicott's notion, cross-identification: the capacity to put oneself in the place of the other based on empathic understanding of similarities of inner experience. The two-year-old's initial role-playing imitation of the departing mother is characterized by the spirit of pure retaliation and reversal — "I'll do to you what you do to me." But gradually the child begins to identify with the mother's subjective experience and realizes, "I could miss you as you miss me," and, therefore, "I know that you could wish to have your own life as I wish to have mine." First shows how, by recognizing such shared experience, the child actually moves from a retaliatory world of control to a world of mutual understanding and shared feeling. This analysis amplifies the idea of object constancy, in which the good object survives the bad experience, by adding the idea of recognizing that the leaving mother is not bad but independent, a person like me. In recognizing this, the child gains not only her own independence (as traditionally emphasized) but also the pleasure of shared understanding.

Looking backward, we can trace the outlines of a developmental trajectory of intersubjective relatedness up to this point. Its core feature is recognizing the similarity of inner experience in tandem with difference. Recognition begins with "We are feeling this feeling" and moves to "I know that you, who are another mind, share this same feeling." In rapprochement, however, a crisis occurs as the child begins to confront difference — "You and I don't want or feel the same thing." The initial response to this discovery is a breakdown of recognition between self and other: "I insist on my way, I refuse to recognize you, I begin to try to coerce you; and therefore I experience your refusal as a reversal: you are coercing me." As in earlier phases, the capacity for mutual recognition must stretch to accommodate the tension of difference, the knowledge of conflicting feelings.

In the third year of life this issue can emerge in symbolic play. The early play at retaliatory reversal may be a kind of empowerment, where the child feels, "I can do to you what you do to me." But then the play expands to include the emotional identification with the other's position and becomes reflexive, so that, as First puts it, "I know you know what I feel." In this sense, the medium of shared feeling remains as important to intersubjectivity in later phases as in early ones, but it is now extended to symbolic understanding of feeling so that "You know what I feel, even when I want or feel the opposite of what you want or feel." This advance in differentiation means that "We can share feelings without my fearing that my feelings are simply your feelings."

The child who can imaginatively entertain both roles — leaving and being left — begins to transcend the complementary form of the mother-child relationship. The complementary structure organizes the relationship of giver and taker, doer and done to, powerful and powerless. It allows us to reverse roles, but not to alter them. In the reversible relationship, each person can play only one role at a time: one person is recognized, the other negated; one is subject, the other object. This complementarity does not dissolve omnipotence but shifts it from one partner to the other. The movement out of the world of complementary power relations into the world of mutual understanding constitutes an important step in the dismantling of omnipotence: power is dissolved rather than transferred back and forth between child and mother in an endless cycle. Again, this movement refers not to a one-time sequence or final accomplishment but to an ongoing tension between complementarity and mutuality.

When mutual recognition is not restored, when shared reality does not survive destruction, then complementary structures and "relating" to the inner object predominate. Because this occurs commonly enough, the intrapsychic, subject-object concept of the mind actually conforms to the dominant mode of internal experience. This is why — notwithstanding our intersubjective potential — the reversible complementarity of subject and object that is conceptualized by intrapsychic theory illuminates so much of the internal world. The principles of mind Freud first analyzed — for example, reversal of opposites like active and passive, the exchangeability or displacement of objects — thus remain indispensable guides to the inner world of objects.

But even when the capacity for recognition is well developed, when the subject can use shared reality and receive the nourishment of "other-than-me substance," the intrapsychic capacities remain. The mind's ability to manipulate, to displace, to reverse, to turn one thing into another, is not a mere negation of reality but the source of mental creativity. Furthermore, when things go well, complementarity is a step on the road to mutuality. The toddler's insistent reciprocity — his efforts to reverse the relationship with the mother, to play at feeding, grooming, and leaving her — is one step in the process of identification that ultimately leads to understanding. Only when this process is disrupted, when the complementary form of the relationship is not balanced by mutual activity, does reversal become entrenched and the relationship become a struggle for power.

The creation of a symbolic space within the infant-mother relationship fosters the dimension of intersubjectivity, a concomitant of mutual understanding. This space, as Winnicott emphasized, is a function not only of the child's play alone in the presence of the mother but also of play between mother and child, beginning with the earliest play of mutual gaze. As we see in First's analysis of play using identification with the leaving mother, the transitional space also evolves within the interaction between mother and child. Within this play, the mother is "related to" in fantasy but at the same time "used" to establish mutual understanding, a pattern that parallels transference play in the analytic situation. In the elaboration of this play the mother can appear as the child's fantasy object and another subject without threatening the child's subjectivity.

The existence of this space is ultimately what makes the intrapsychic capacities creative rather than destructive; perhaps it is another way of referring to the tension between using and relating. Using—that is, recognizing—implies the capacity to transcend complementary structures, but not the absence of them. It does not mean the disappearance of fantasy or negation but that "destruction becomes the unconscious backcloth for love of a real object" (Winnicott 1969b, p. 111). It means a balance of destruction with recognition. In the broadest sense, internal fantasy is always eating up or negating external reality—"While I am loving you I am all the time destroying you in (unconscious) fantasy" (p. 106). The loved one is continually being destroyed, but its survival means that we can eat our reality and have it too. From the intersubjective standpoint, all fantasy is the negation of the real other, whether its content is negative or idealized—just as, from the intrapsychic view, external reality is simply that which is internalized as fantasy. The ongoing interplay of destruction and recognition is a dialectic between fantasy and external reality.

The original challenge for interpersonal and object relations theories was to eliminate the notion of a biological drive underpinning destructiveness and yet find a place for the destructive and reality-negating forces in mental life. My exposition of the crisis of the self is meant, in part, to answer this challenge. If we want to claim that relations with others are essential to the self, then we cannot help but acknowledge aggression as a necessary moment of psychic life. Many relational thinkers have argued that aggression is not a primary but a secondary response to deprivation or frustration. But this is true only from the point of view of one-person psychology, of intrapsychic experience, which defines that which frustrates us—the will of the other—as inessential, external, not intrinsic to the self. From an intersubjective standpoint, the clash of two wills is inherent in subject-subject relations, an ineluctable moment that every self has to confront. (Any parent who has daily experience with two toddlers grabbing the same toy and screeching "Mine!" is bound to wonder whether it was naive to abandon drive theory; only the most utopian anarchist could deny that this crisis is one that everyone who has equals must confront.) Of course, we may theoretically distinguish between reactions to "unnecessary" frustration and loss and this sort of aggression, even if in practice the lines between them sometimes smudge.

The intersubjective analysis of the crisis of recognition may help to counter the idealism that otherwise afflicts relational theories — the tendency to throw out with the drives the fundamental psychic place of aggression. I suspect that we need this fundamental acceptance to tolerate and work with aggression in the clinical situation, that otherwise we may be tempted to see it as defensive, "bad," or inauthentic. In any event, respect for the inner world — including the "bad" — leads me to prefer a theoretical perspective in which intersubjectivity rivals but does not defeat the intrapsychic. Such a theoretical approach can then explicitly try to account for the imbalance between intrapsychic and intersubjective structures without succumbing to the temptation to make the inner world a mere reflection of or reaction to the outer.

In the analytic process, the effort to share the productions of fantasy changes the status of fantasy itself, moving it from inner reality to intersubjective communication. The fantasy object who is being related to or destroyed and the usable other who is "there to receive the communication" and be loved complement each other. What we find in the good hour is a momentary balance between intrapsychic and intersubjective dimensions, a sustained tension or rapid movement between the patient's experience of us as inner material and as the recognizing other. Suspension of the conflict between the two experiences reflects the establishment of a transitional space in which the otherness of the analyst can be ignored as well as recognized.[2] The experience of a space that allows both creative exploration within omnipotence and acknowledgment of an understanding other is, in part, what is therapeutic about the relationship.

The restoration of balance between the intrapsychic and the intersubjective in the psychoanalytic process should not be construed as an adaptation that reduces fantasy to reality; rather, it is practice in the sustaining of contradiction. When the tension of sustaining contradiction breaks down, as it frequently does, the intersubjective structures—mutuality, simultaneity, and paradox—are subordinated to complementary structures. The breakdown of tension between self and other in favor of relating as subject and object is a common fact of mental life. For that matter, breakdown is a common feature within intersubjective relatedness—what counts is the ability to restore or repair the relationship. As Beebe and Lachmann have proposed, one of the main principles of the early dyad is that relatedness is characterized not by continuous harmony but by continuous disruption and repair (Beebe and Lachmann 1988, 1994; Tronick 1989).

Thus an intersubjective theory can explore the development of mutual recognition without equating breakdown with pathology. It does not require a normative ideal of balance that equates breakdown with failure and the accompanying phenomena—internalization, fantasy, aggression—with pathology. If the clash of two wills is an inherent part of intersubjective relations, then no perfect environment can take the sting from the encounter with otherness. The question becomes how the inevitable elements of negation are processed. It is "good

2. Perhaps for this reason Winnicott chooses to begin "The Use of an Object" with a reminder that it is essential to accept the paradox that the baby both discovers and creates transitional phenomena, that is, they exist both outside and inside.

enough" that the inward movement of negating reality and creating fantasy should eventually be counterbalanced by an outward movement of recognizing the outside. To claim anything more for intersubjectivity would invite a triumph of the external, a terrifying psychic vacuity, an end to creativity altogether. A relational psychoanalysis should leave room for the messy, intrapsychic side of creativity and aggression; it is the contribution of the intersubjective view that may give these elements a more hopeful cast, showing destruction to be the Other of recognition.

2 / Sameness and Difference: An "Overinclusive" View of Gender Constitution

The idea of gender development has of necessity been linked to the notion of coming to terms with difference. What has changed in contemporary psychoanalysis is the meaning of sexual difference. Assimilating the meaning of sexual difference(s) and assuming a position in relation to it/them are no longer seen as being triggered by the discovery of anatomical facts. The way in which perceptions of anatomy and the body come to *figure* difference is now a matter for further exploration. Psychoanalytic assumptions about the character of gender difference, however, have not been wholly liberated from the naturalizing tendency in Freud's thought, although they exist in a more covert and subtle form: the tendency to view the realization of difference as if it were more significant than, and detached from, the realization of likeness. The implicit assumption in differentiation theory is that acknowledging difference has a higher value, is a later achievement, and is more difficult

An earlier version of this essay appeared in *Psychoanalytic Inquiry* 15 (1995):125–42. Used by permission.

than recognizing likeness. The neglected point is that the difficulty lies in assimilating difference without repudiating likeness — that is, in straddling the space between the opposites. It is easy enough to give up one side of a polarity in order to oscillate toward the other side. What is difficult is to attain a notion of difference, being unlike, without giving up a sense of commonality, of being a "like" human being.

Some time ago Chodorow (1979) suggested that men characteristically overvalue difference and depreciate commonality because of their more precarious sense of masculinity and repudiation of the mother. To conceptualize a tension between sameness and difference, rather than a binary opposition that values one and depreciates the other, is thus part of the effort to critique the masculinist orientation of psychoanalysis. But to deconstruct that binary opposition between sameness and difference — rather than simply to critique the overvaluation of difference or to revalue sameness — requires us to address the problem of identity as well. For the term *identity* pertains in contemporary gender-differentiation theory inasmuch as it equates difference with the boundary between identities. That conception of difference has been criticized in recent feminist thought in favor of a notion of multiple differences and unstable identifications.

To move beyond a discourse of opposites requires the notion of something more plural, decentered, than is implied by the simple axis of sameness-difference, the idea of the one Difference. The notion of a singular Difference as a dividing line suggests that on either side of that line exists identity, everything on that side is homogeneous with everything else. By that logic identity is destiny, like has only to identify with like, and acknowledging difference means respecting the boundary between what one is and what one cannot be. The idea of gender identity implies an inevitability, a coherence, a singularity, and a uniformity that belies psychoanalytic notions of fantasy, sexuality, and the unconscious (May 1986; Goldner 1991; Dimen 1991).

Although I intend to use this critique of identity, I wish to first clarify an essential distinction between identity and identification. In giving up the notion of identity, reified as thing, one need not (and should not) throw out the notion of identification, as internal psychic process. One need not assume that the process of identification always falls along one side of the axis of sameness-difference. To attend to the process of assimilating differences and of learning to know "the difference," it is not necessary to privilege Difference. To define that process as reflecting the work of culture — that is, as organized by discursive systems rather than by the innate, presocial imperatives of the psyche — does not in itself reveal the complexity of that work. To point out the reification of gender only confronts us with its mysterious persistence as a demarcation of psychic experience that is at once firm and resilient but highly volatile in its location and content (see Harris 1991); like bacteria, gender categories often seem able to mutate just enough to produce resistant strains.

To begin an investigation of identifications that takes the feminist critique into account, let us review some current psychoanalytic thinking about gender development. I will discuss some of the prominent positions in the contemporary theory, which can be traced from Stoller's work on gender identity to Fast's "differentiation model." I want both to make use of this theory and to critique it, at the same time preserving its notable observations and pushing it past the notion of identity. I will follow the axis of sameness-difference and highlight the changes in the contemporary view of the early development of gender identifications.

In presenting this outline, I recognize that feminist theory has raised as many objections to the notion of developmental order as to the idea of identity. But the developmental narrative to which these objections refer is an antiquated oedipal model (circa 1933) that is only one of the stories that inform current psychoanalytic practice. Before subjecting it to criticism, we ought to differentiate the contemporary narrative of gender development from Freud's, or even the later revisions by Stoller. Furthermore, as the category of identification continues to be central to all theorizing about gender, the contemporary narrative on how gender categories take hold in the psyche remains instructive. In the past decade or so, there have been some interesting insights into the formulation of sexual difference outside the oedipal structure. These insights enlarge our potential understanding of the many identifications and experiences, conscious and unconscious, that exceed the rigid notion of identity. And finally, it is necessary to retain a tie, however elastic, to the observational world in which, whatever we infer about the unconscious, it is apparent that children really do represent and assimilate some things before others, are preoccupied with certain conflicts at one time more than another, as the idea of phase suggests.[1] It is the normative use of this notion, as I shall discuss, that disparages earlier in favor of later. But this disparagement is not logically necessary, any more than is the disparagement of subjects and verbs because they are learned earlier than adverbs, of walking because it precedes skipping.

One previously undervalued, if not denied, aspect of gender

1. We may wish to exchange the idea of *phase* as a self-enclosed, exclusive geological layer for a sense that psychic events overlap and recur, are not merely successive but often coincident, are usually known retroactively through appearance rather than in "pure culture." Still, retaining a flexible idea of phase has the advantage of allowing a notion of complexes which, if they do not remain temporally organized after their initial introduction, still retain a structural connection. The idea of development has to be suspended and yet preserved — Lacan, who is often cited by feminist critics, did no less.

development that I will highlight is the coming together of likeness with difference — in particular, the identification with the parent understood to be of a different sex. "Identification with difference" (see Chapter 4), an intentionally paradoxical formulation, is meant to suggest an identification that crosses the line that demarks what we are supposedly like, the boundary that encloses the identical. Recent theorizing by Fast (1984) shows how children use cross-sex identifications to formulate important parts of their self representations as well as to imaginatively elaborate their fantasies about erotic relations between the sexes. Fast's theory of gender differentiation (1984) argues that children are initially bisexual, reintrepreting the idea of bisexuality to mean not a constitutional, biological anlage but a position of identifying with both parents (1990). In the preoedipal phase children are "overinclusive": they believe they can have or be everything. They do not yet recognize the exclusivity of the anatomical difference; they want what the other sex has, not *instead* of but in *addition* to what they have.

I will outline how current theorizing sees gender difference as developmentally integrated, bringing together my own observations with Fast's views, Stoller's work, and that of some of Stoller's critics. I will propose a new periodization, which delineates four main phases in early gender development: (*1*) nominal gender identification, (*2*) early differentiation of identifications in the context of separation-individuation, (*3*) the preoedipal overinclusive phase, and (*4*) the oedipal phase. The premise of this differentiation perspective, as will be evident, is virtually the opposite of the position that genital difference is the motor of developing gender and sexual identity (see Roiphe and Galenson 1981). Rather, it embarks from the position, articulated clearly by Person and Ovesey (1983), according to which gender differentiation, evolving through separation conflicts, early losses and identifications, defines and gives weight to the genital difference, which then assumes great (if not exclusive) symbolic significance in the representation of gender experience and relations. However, my scheme is "overinclusive," rereading critically and integrating many contributions of earlier psychosexual theory.

An Overinclusive View of Development

Stoller (1968), as we know, offered a new conceptualization of the earliest phase of gender development as the formation of core gender identity in the first year and a half of life: a felt conviction of being male or female, which later expands to the conviction of belonging to one or the other group. Rather than referring to this as identity, we might call it nominal gender identification. Perhaps because the conclusions of infancy research were not available to Stoller when he postulated his notion of core gender identity, he was not sure how to formulate a kind of "primordial representation" (Stoller 1973) appropriate to the first year of life. He thought that identification and incorporation were not appropriate categories, for Stoller subscribed to the then-current view in which the mother was considered not yet outside or separate and therefore not able to be taken in. But since Daniel Stern (1985) presented his notions of an infant who begins differentiating mother almost from birth and of presymbolic interaction (representation of interactions generalized or RIGS; see also Beebe 1990), we can posit a process of nominal gender identification, rather than a product, core gender identity; we can picture this identification as developing through concrete representations of self-body and self-other body interactions, which are retroactively defined as gendered (Fast 1984).

Stoller by no means postulated core gender identity as a final achievement of masculinity or femininity. He acknowledged that the "sense of belonging to a sex becomes complicated" by later conflicts and fantasies, anxiety and defense, complications that render masculinity and femininity far more ambiguous than maleness and femaleness (1973). Indeed, he argued that only if the male child separates from his mother in the separation-individuation phase — "disidentifies" in Greenson's term — can he develop that "non-core gender identity we call masculinity." He did not offer a full picture of the preoedipal period, however, and both he and Greenson use the notion of disidentification to imply that the male child fully gives up his identification with mother. I hold, rather, that at this point the child still identifies with both parents, who are only beginning to be partially, concretely differentiated. Given this persistence of multiple identifications, the idea that the self identifies as belonging to a sex should not be equated with the idea of an unambiguous and coherent identity. On the contrary, the core sense of belonging does not organize all gender experience. Core or nominal gender identification makes sense only if we conceptualize it as a background for future gender ambiguity and tension, a repetitive baseline against which all the other instruments play different, often conflicting or discordant, lines.[2]

Sometime in the second year of life, particularly with the advent of symbolic representation in the second half of the second year, the next phase of gender constitution begins, at the level of identifications. Person and Ovesey (1983) refer to this

2. To make *core* and *nominal* equivalent is, I am aware, highly contradictory, for they are rooted in different metaphors, one geometrical, the other linguistic. Because this early identification figures as unknown quantity, I prefer the idea of "nominal"; but this early identification may, indeed, be central, so I do not wish to prematurely dismiss the notion of "core." Assignment or appellation, moreover, from which we derive the idea of "nominal," may at times be violently rejected as a "false" surface by those who experience their "core" to be other (transsexuals, e.g.) — a phenomenon too compelling to explain away, except to note that other identifications, other early experiences may be equally constitutive of the presymbolic "core."

as gender role identity to distinguish it from core gender identity: masculine or feminine self-image rather than male and female designations. (Again, "gender role identification" would be a better term.) Gender role identity is defined as a psychological achievement occurring in the conflictual context of separation-individuation. Person and Ovesey disagree with Stoller's theorem that boys must separate more than girls, arguing rather that conflict around separation has a gender marker for boys. Coates's work on gender disorder (Coates, Friedman, and Wolfe 1991) supports this critique of Stoller, disputing the notion that transsexuals have difficulty separating from maternal symbiosis. She finds rather that maternal withdrawal can inspire a profound melancholic identification, which is manifested as excessive femininity in boys as well as in girls. The upshot of this analysis is to emphasize dynamic issues like separation anxiety or envy rather than to see disidentification from mother as an inherently pathogenic process.

At this same point of early separation, I have proposed, we see before and alongside object love something we might call identificatory love, a love that has conventionally appeared first in the relationship to the rapprochement father (Benjamin 1986, 1988, 1991). Following Abelin (1980), I have stressed that in traditional gender arrangements the father (or other masculine representation) plays a crucial role in representing separation, agency, and desire in the rapprochement phase. In contrast to Abelin, though, I have argued that ideally children of both sexes continue to identify with both parents and that the rapprochement father is therefore as important for girls as for boys. In this phase, the parents begin to be differentiated in the child's mind, but the child continues to elaborate both identifications as aspects of self. Traditionally, the mother, the source of goodness, as Klein put it, is experienced as the complementary other, a precursor of the outside love object, whereas the father is sought as an object to be like. The mother has represented holding, attachment, and caretaking while father has represented the outside world, exploration, freedom — a "knight in shining armor," says Mahler (cited in Abelin 1980). This parental constellation has created a distinct structural position for the rapprochement father, a function that may be played by other figures who represent separate subjectivity. Indeed, I would argue that this position is so psychically and culturally important, so distinct from that of the oedipal father, that it persists despite variations in the role and gender of those who represent it.

The function of the father at this point, as Freud (1921, 1925) originally stated and as Blos (1984) and Tyson (1986) have reiterated, is dyadic, not triadic, that is to say, not rivalrous or forbidding, like the oedipal father. He does not so much represent the one who can exclusively love mother (as the child still imagines doing directly) as he embodies the desire for the exciting outside. What I wish to underscore is the importance of a second adult, not necessarily a male or a father, with whom the child can form a second dyad. The key feature of this person, or position, is not yet that he or she loves the mother and seals the triangle, but that he or she creates the second vector, which points outward and on which the triangle can be formed. Identification with a second other as a "like subject" makes the child imaginatively able to represent the desire for the outside world.[3]

3. My conception of the preoedipal father has overlapping characteristics with the imaginary father whom Kristeva (1987) describes, the father who helps the child to "abject" (separate from) the mother. She sees this metaphorical object of idealization as a basis of transference distinct from merger or maternal satisfaction. But Kristeva's emphasis on the ternary structure seems to distract from the child's direct relation to the father. Although she appropriates Freud's contention that identification is the first tie to the object, an immediate relation rather than an effect of lost love, and she recognizes that loving and being like, narcissism and object, are not as distinct as they appear to be, she does not follow through. For her the father represents first the mother's desire for someone other than the child,

As a consequence of this representation of desire, the new feature associated with this phase, its legacy to adult erotic life, is identificatory love. Identificatory love remains associated with certain aspects of idealization and excitement throughout life.[4] This identification with the ideal has a defensive function, masking the loss of control over mother that would otherwise be felt intensely at this point. It is a way of sustaining the practicing grandiosity that would otherwise be challenged. But it is not only defensive, insofar as the ideal father serves symbolically to represent longings that the child may one day hope to realize, as well as the freedom, agency, and contact with the outside world of other people that partially compensate for loss of control.

The idea that the child represents her or his own desire by identifying with an idealized figure who is imagined as the subject of desire has wider repercussions. It was on the basis of such a formulation — that the ego constitutes itself by taking the Other as its ideal — that Lacan (1977) argued that the ego is necessarily alienated. It misrecognizes itself in the ideal, in the image of the unified figure in the mirror; it takes the other or an

---

rather than the child's desire for someone other than the mother. The child is thus less active, without her or his own desire except in reaction to the mother's desire. Would not this condition itself indicate lack of separation?

4. Identificatory love is related to what Freud referred to in his distinction (1914) between narcissistic and anaclitic object choice. Why not use that terminology? Contradictions emerge because, as Borch-Jacobsen (1989) points out, narcissism is, strictly speaking, not love of an outside object. The phrase "narcissistic object love" would be an oxymoron, whereas terminologically, identificatory love can be paired with object love. If identificatory love *is* love and is a relationship to an outside other, then it is arguably a less "narcissistic" relationship than the anaclitic relation, which "leans on" the ego instincts — that is, the original attachment figure, source of goodness, in Freud's words "the woman who feeds him" (1914, p. 88). In other words, identificatory love first shows up in relation not to "the same" but to "the one who is different from the first." The point Freud got right here was that women engage in "narcissistic" — that is, identificatory — love when they love in a man the ideal self they would have wished to be. But, oddly, he failed to see that this might be less regressive, more exciting, more of an "object love," than loving the person who feeds you.

imaginary construct for itself. In this sense the subject is produced, "subjected," at the very moment it imagines it is finding itself. I have suggested (Benjamin 1988) that, indeed, the identification of self with the ideal other constitutes the point of alienation in recognition. But the acts of creating the ideal, forming an identificatory bond, and actively pursuing the relationship with the beloved figure are, in effect, the subject's own. In the experience we call "subject of desire," the subject casts out the line of identification as well as reeling in the other at the end of the hook. It is the casting outward that constitutes desire, and the recognition that both I and the other can do this symmetrically that creates a shared identificatory bond, "like subjects." If the placing of the ideal in the other, a process meant to avoid the conflict of dependency, reinstalls dependency on otherness at the heart of the subject, that is problematic only if we understand the subject to be somehow originally independent, enclosed, and identical with itself. (Or, we could say, proof of this dependency is newsworthy only if one is still crusading against unresolved aspirations to independent identity.) If not, we accept that the activity of identification and identificatory love may give the lie to identity but make possible the position as a subject of desire.

Unlike Abelin (1980), Roiphe and Galenson (1981), and others who have emphasized girls' "castration reaction," I am convinced that identificatory love of the father (or the position of the "second") is important to the girl in her effort to define herself as a subject of desire. This idea is one illustration of the way that "identification with difference" is crucial (see Chapter 4). The girl, too, needs to use the fantasy of power to inspire efforts to attain a sense of autonomy over her own body and the ability to move into a wider world. Likewise, a girl's identification with "masculinity" primarily reflects not a reaction to a sense of castration but love and admiration of father.

But the relationship to father is not identical for both sexes. Identificatory love of the father figure for boys not only supports separation but also confirms the achievement of masculinity as a naturalized "male destiny." This gives the relationship with father a desperate urgency, often visible in the analytic encounter, as if it were the bulwark of the boy's representation of gender as identity (his sense of self-cohesion, as Kohut's model [1977] states, implicitly aligning the father with the self-cohering object). In patriarchal convention, sons are not only oedipal rivals but also more important to a father's narcissism. A stronger mutual attraction between father and son is often fostered by the father himself, and this promotes recognition through identification, a special erotic relationship. As I have written elsewhere, the practicing toddler's "love affair with the world" turns into a homoerotic love affair with the father, who represents the world. The boy is in love with his ideal. This homoerotic, identificatory love serves as the boy's vehicle of establishing masculinity, both defensively and creatively; it confirms his sense of himself as subject of desire. Of course, identificatory love must be reciprocated for identification to "stick"—it is not loss of love, not asymmetry, but mutuality that furthers this kind of identification. Its baseline is the father's own narcissistic pride, when he identifies with his son and says, "You can be like me," or when the validating mother says, "You are just like your Dad."

I should make it clear that the rapprochement father is a kind of first love, but not "the one and only" paradigm of identificatory love, particularly for girls. Later on, for instance, adolescent girls often develop this sort of love for a woman who represents their ideal, a "second" mother. Godwin's novel *The Finishing School* describes a girl's adolescent crush on a woman who represents independence and access to the world, who is meant to compensate for a sexually dependent mother. And although identificatory love of the father figure, under traditional gender arrangements, has had this special representational meaning, of course the mother remains an important figure of identification for boys as well as girls. Furthermore, although girls know they are female like mother, it is an effort to become feminine like her. Insofar as the rapprochement phase confronts children with the difference between mother's power and their own, between grandiose aspirations and reality, "femininity," like "masculinity," appears as an ideal, only partly attainable, if not in conflict with affirming one's own desire. In the analytic situation, women often seek women analysts who precisely embody the subject of desire with whom to identify, and with whom oedipal competition and phallic aggression can be integrated. Women analysts, in turn, repeatedly discuss their difficulty in being that subject: in separating themselves from the ideal of maternal femininity that enjoins giving, receiving, holding, mirroring the other's desire but abjures penetrating interpretation, opposition or conflict, or desire on one's own behalf (see Schachtel 1986). Many have the greatest difficulty with the aggressive spin on the will's assertion, the legacy of the toddler's ruthless "I want!" or insistent "No!"

It is also important to reiterate that the boy does not need to forgo identification with mother so early unless difficulties in separation lead to an early, defensive repudiation. The child has no sense of mutual exclusivity, does not need to choose between mother and father. As Stoller pointed out (1973), the boy's preoedipal love for the mother is certainly not heterosexual, it is not strictly speaking object love — love for someone different or outside. It is, however, more complementary than identificatory; that is, it is based on interlocking asymmetrical roles that can be reversed. Giver and receiver alternate rather than symmetrically forming "a love of parallels," as Dinesen said of her love for Finch-Hatton (Thurman 1981). It is in this sense that mother has traditionally been love object rather than "like subject" — an opposition, as I have reiterated, that need not devolve upon real men and women in the present.

There is, furthermore, a difference between inside and outside, between the one more familiar and the one more different, the love for the security of nearness and the love that aims for the shining star. If father is identified with in a special way because he is "different" from the primary object — a subject, not a source, of goodness — then identification with mother is with "sameness," a kind of "primordial" identification, as suggested by Stoller (1973).

As long as the primary caretaker is the mother — or perhaps even as long as the maternal body is culturally instituted as the essential metaphor of this first relation — this allocation of sameness and difference must initially be the same for both sexes. In this traditional allocation, father has meant the outside object who represents "difference." This representation of Difference has been so important, so embedded in the culture, that it usually continues to be effective as an ideal even when a person not defined as father occupies the structural position of "second other." Indeed, it is so constitutive of masculinity as to give this second other a paternal quality even when played by a woman. At most, the absence of a defined or literal father figure means that a more complex tension develops between the experience and the cultural ideal of relationships.

Let us turn now to the preoedipal, overinclusive phase. What becomes of identificatory love, especially if it is directed toward the sexual other? As we have seen, the positive elaboration of characteristics that may later be yielded to the different other still proceeds through identification with difference. These characteristics depend in part on the parental validation of the identificatory love that informs cross-sex identification. In the preoedipal overinclusive phase, as denoted by Fast (1984), children not only identify with both parents but begin to symbolize genital meanings and assimilate unconsciously the gestural and behavioral vocabulary supplied by the culture to express masculinity and femininity. Now recognizing certain basic distinctions between masculinity and femininity, children continue to try, through bodily mimesis, to imaginatively elaborate both options within themselves. A thirty-month-old girl may imitate her older brother's play with action figures in order to assimilate symbolic masculinity, the phallic repertoire of colliding, penetrating, invading, and blocking. A boy of twenty-four months may insist that he has a vagina, but at three years, more aware of external anatomy, he might instead claim to have a baby inside his tummy, elaborating a fantasy of receiving, holding, and expelling. This phase also shows a mixing of identifications in rapid succession: a three-and-one-half-year-old girl, jealous of the girl her older brother plays with, strides up to her and flexes the muscles on her own raised arms, saying, "I'm stronger than you." A few minutes later, to create yet another forceful impression, she insists that her mother dress her in her ballerina costume. Among the early psychoanalysts, Klein (1928, 1945) most clearly recognized the child's need to identify with and make symbolic use of all the organs and parental capacities, including those fantasized as part of the mother-father interaction.

To the extent that the child imaginatively identifies without yet realizing the impossibility of acquiring certain capacities and organs, envy is not a dominant motive. But gradually the overinclusive period becomes characterized by envy and ongoing protest against increasing realization of gender difference, says Fast (1984). At this point, castration represents for both sexes the loss of the opposite sex capacities and genitals. This protest is not completely symmetrical: for boys the focus is usually on the capacity to bear a baby, whereas for girls the coveted thing is the penis (Fast 1984). But the sexes are parallel in their insistence on being everything, their elaboration of complementarity as opposites held within the self, and their protest against limits.

The oedipal phase, beginning toward the end of the fourth year, might be considered gender differentiation proper, when the complementary opposites are attributed to self and to other, respectively. In other words, the dynamic of renunciation — abandoning hope of fulfilling identificatory love of one parent — might be seen as the road to object love: loving the object as an outside figure who embodies what the self does not, may not, or cannot. But this construction raises an important question about the prevalence of the heterosexual model. Is the radical oedipal separation between love object and like subject equally characteristic of homosexual object choice, or is it a specific feature of heterosexuality? If, as the idea of the negative oedipal supposes, all children follow a pattern of identifying unconsciously with the opposite-sex parent and loving the same-sex one, then the oedipal separation of love and like may be fragile or contradictory (see Borch-Jacobsen 1988). In any event, we must ask whether the homosexual positions reflect a simple "inversion" of the heterosexual: is the parent of the same nominal gender simply experienced as less the same, or is a different relationship between identificatory and object love formulated? Is not the more complex intertwining of the two tendencies more common than is often supposed?

The delineation I have offered serves primarily to reformulate the notion of how the heterosexual positions are taken up. But it may be safe to say that complementarity becomes the oedipal preoccupation for all children, and the culturally dominant formulation of gender complementarity is internalized as an ideal, however much it may contradict the complexity of the individual's desires and identifications. Complementarity conveys a distance — having rather than being — that carries a possible threat. For to "be" something, to act it in one's own body, is still a crucial mechanism of maintaining closeness. In the early phase of oedipal differentiation, a three-and-one-half-year-old boy who had earlier expressed wishes to be like his mother began to insist on calling himself Mickey and her Minnie — as in Mouse. He would say lovingly, "Isn't this a nice day we're havin', Minnie?" He explained this one night at bedtime, saying, "You're a girl and I'm a boy, but we're both mice; we're both little." Complementarity, then, did not have to fully abrogate likeness; a sense of belonging to the same species compensated for the loss of being alike in gender. Another possible interpretation is that the boy, unable to accept the "double difference," as Chasseguet-Smirgel calls it, could take in the gender difference only by denying the generational one. Yet another approach is to postulate that all identifications, especially those that psychoanalysis calls successful, work in this way. By the age of four, this piece of reality is accepted, and the complementary modality of having — mastery, possession of objects — becomes pervasive, a defense against a barely tolerated loss.

The early oedipal phase (at and just before age four) is usually more defensive, characterized by a rigid definition of gender complementarity and — as Freud noted of boys but overlooked in girls — by scornful repudiation of the opposite sex. In this phase castration anxiety refers to the loss of one's own genitals, again acknowledged by Freud only for boys. As Mayer (1985) has pointed out, however, the fear of losing one's own genitals is crucial for girls at this point as well and is accompanied by sexual chauvinism, insistence that "everyone must be just like me," fear and repudiation of the other. This chauvinism is characterized by the attitude that, to paraphrase the famous dictum about winning, "What I have is not everything, but it is the *only thing* (worth having)." Freud's theory of phallic monism

(Chasseguet-Smirgel 1976) exemplified this dictum perfectly. As Horney (1926) rightly pointed out, Freud's theory corresponds to the thinking of the oedipal boy who believes that girls have "nothing." Envy, feelings of loss, and resentment spur both the repudiation and the idealization of the opposite sex at this point. Sometimes love and longing for the lost other predominate, sometimes rivalry and repudiation.

Conventionally, during the later oedipal phase the rigid insistence on complementarity and the repudiation of the other are ameliorated (Fast 1984) as the fantasy of object love comes to compensate for narcissistic loss. But oedipal love is both a resolution and a perpetuation of mourning. One cannot yet embody the ideal of femininity or masculinity that mother and father represent, and one cannot yet "possess" the other body in love: one can neither be nor have. In my view, the unaccepted mourning for what one will never *be*—especially the boy's inability to face the loss entailed in not being the mother, even to acknowledge envy of the feminine—has particularly negative repercussions, often more profound and culturally pervasive, if less obvious, than the classically recognized oedipal frustration of not having mother. The method of dealing with this loss is as much a matter of cultural mediation as of individual object relationships. Because identifications with parents are now supplemented by secondary identifications, the tempering of complementarity and repudiation varies according to the flexibility of the culture and the peer group regarding cross-gender identifications.

Here I want to note an important difference between early identificatory love and later oedipal love identifications. Identificatory love has been wrongly assimilated to the boy's negative oedipus complex, a linkage that conflates the boy's homoerotic wish to be loved by father as like him with the heteroerotic wish to be to father as mother is. These are actually obverse relationships to father. The negative Oedipus, I suggest, represents a movement from identification to object love, paralleling the positive oedipal movement from identification to object love of the opposite sex.[5] However, in the negative oedipal case the boy renounces identification with father, not because of the ineluctable dictates of gender but because of parental impediments to the identificatory paternal bond. In other words, thwarted identificatory love turns into ideal love, a submissive or hostile tie to a powerful, admired father who emasculates the boy rather than confirming his masculinity. This impediment frequently arises when the father is too far outside the mother-child dyad and, prematurely oedipalizing his stance toward his son, is too rivalrous or too afraid of his own sadistic impulses to be tender. This transformation then presents and is often analyzed as a negative oedipal wish for a passive relation with father.

Blos (1984) has also argued for a reinterpretation of the negative oedipal stance in terms of the wish for the dyadic father, which he sees as requiring resolution to allow heterosexual wishes to be authentic. Blos's position poses an important challenge to a superficial notion of heterosexuality, which places it in opposition to homoerotic currents. The "father hunger" shown by sons of absent fathers is primarily a reaction to lack of homoerotic love. In heterosexual men it becomes an impediment to loving women, not simply because there is no "role

5. Here, too, the question arises as to whether "opposite" sex means the parent whose nominal gender is different or whether it can be the parent perceived as same. This issue pertains not only to homosexuality. After all, the negative oedipal wish to be loved by the father and like mother is called homosexual, but is a heteroerotic wish. Conversely, the girl's wish to be recognized as a like subject by the father has a strong homoerotic component: sometimes an explicit fantasy of being the son is later expressed in the wish to be the partner to a male homosexual or in a heterosexual love in which she feels she both is one of the boys and loves the boys. In this case, admiring a man is not coded as being "feminine," does not mean playing the mirroring role to his phallic power. The real question, as Butler (1990) points out, is whether psychoanalysis leaves room for homosexuality at all — a love that does not mean identifying with the position of opposite sex to the partner.

model" but because the erotic energy is tied to the frustrated wish for recognition from the father. In cultures dominated by this frustrated father-son erotic, women become valuable not as sources of inner satisfaction but as signifiers of male prowess, as currency in the exchange of power. Frequently, the thwarting of paternal identificatory love pushes the boy to deny his identificatory love of the mother on whom he depends too exclusively, spurring an exaggerated repudiation of femininity.

Then, too, the boy's repudiation of femininity may well represent the next move in a chain that includes the mother's inability to satisfy her identificatory love of her father, which has led her to sacrifice desire and early grandiosity. In her admiration of her son, she unconsciously communicates her feelings as the daughter whose identificatory love of the father became an ideal love of the one she could not be. Perpetuating this ideal love, she projects her desire and grandiosity onto her male child. Thus the boy's gender splitting may be set up before the oedipal, in rapprochement, when an idealized and inaccessible father is paired with a mother who views her son as her ideal masculine self. And so we can reinterpret the sense of Freud's (1933) assertion that a mother's love of her firstborn son was the only unambivalent love. Freud gave the mother a son to love in place of the phallus she could not have. To the mother was granted fulfillment of the wish for identificatory love, not in relation to her father but in ideal love of her son; to the son was given the grandiosity that is mirrored by the mother who renounced it. But Freud's story also bequeathed the son an ideal love — a forever unrequited search for identificatory love of the father who has cast him out as a murderous rival. This may be the great triangle of identificatory love, replayed endlessly in stories of women's submission to and sacrifice for heroes who leave them to follow the quest for the paternal grail, the father's recognition.

Toward a Critique of Gender Complementarity

The first conclusion I want to draw from the foregoing is that to the degree that the characteristics of the other have been lovingly incorporated through identification in the overinclusive phase, loss can be ameliorated by intimacy, and the sequelae of the oedipal phase can be informed more by other-love than by repudiation/idealization. The acceptance of one's own limits and the ability to love what is different in the other are not compromised by the previous integration of opposite-sex identifications. On the contrary, as Fast suggests, if the individual does not get stuck in the rigid complementarity of the early oedipal phase, the tendency to denigrate what cannot be had may give way to an easier familiarity with opposite-sex characteristics later on.

I diverge from Fast, however, where she insists on the necessity of renouncing what belongs to the other and relinquishing the narcissism of bisexuality. I would rather speculate that elaborating opposite-sex feelings/behavior/attitudes under the umbrella of one's own narcissism persists as a preconscious or unconscious capacity (Aron 1995; Bassin 1994), which comprehends both cross-sex identification and the ability to represent and symbolize the role of the other in sexual relations. For most individuals, this capacity may be a relatively benign form of omnipotence. Aron suggests that it may be more helpful to think of the grandiose, narcissistic aspiration to bisexual completeness as a position that is a source of creativity — as something not to be relinquished but rather to be maintained alongside and modified by the more differentiated positions.[6] Likewise, the wish to

6. In Kleinian theory, the notion of position rather than phase allows for more flexible usage. Thus Aron points out that a notion of positions, which can be maintained simultaneously, parallels recent Klein interpretations that insist that the schizoid position should remain in dialectical tension with the depressive position rather than being replaced by it (see Eigen, 1985; Ogden, 1986).

attain commonality in the form of identificatory love should alternate with enjoyment of difference in object love. Identification could then be used to ratify sameness and/or to create commonality as a bridge across difference.

The idea that the child renounces the other's prerogatives in the oedipal phase seems to misconstrue gender identity as a final achievement, a cohesive, stable system, rather than an unattainable oedipal ideal with which the self constantly struggles. As Goldner (1991) has pointed out, the relation between the ideal self-representation and actual self-experience is an uneasy tension at best, taxed by rigid and contradictory prescriptions of complementarity. A gendered self-representation is continually destabilized by conflicting mandates and identifications, requiring a capacity for living with contradiction that is in no way culturally supported (Goldner 1991). A psychoanalytic posture requires recognition of these contradictions — the ability, as Harris (1991) has shown, to divine the multiplicity of positions beneath the appearance of singularity in object choice or identifications and to see gender experience as both tenacious and fragile, reified substance and dissolving insubstantial. This posture also means, as Dimen (1991) has argued, deconstructing the reified gender dichotomies and thinking of gender in transitional terms, leaving a world of fixed boundaries with uncrossable borders for a transitional territory in which the conventional opposites create movable walls and pleasurable tension.

The use of a developmental trajectory may seem to imply a telos, and in this case it might be thought that identification is simply the basis for object love, that reaching an oedipal position is the ultimate goal of development, that we need not look any further. Despite my argument for integrating overinclusiveness with complementarity, the alignment of inclusiveness with early narcissism might be misconstrued to privilege later sexual complementarity and object love over early inclusiveness and identificatory love. Such a construction would reflect the pejorative notions about narcissism implicit in some psychoanalytic thinking. Alternatively, the inclusive view could lead to recognizing identificatory love and object love as frequently coincident, rather than as mutually exclusive, and indeed, could cause mutual exclusivity to appear problematic. From this view follow both a positive revaluing of narcissism and a questioning of heterosexual complementarity as the goal of development.

Thus, as I contended earlier, a developmental view of differentiation need not posit a normative goal of sexual identity, nor must we abandon all empirically based reflections on development to avoid normative positions. The extraction of such positions from notions of development reflects the acceptance of unrelated and unsupportable assumptions: that earlier is more fundamental but later is better (more developed), that development is unilinear, that it is desirable for all conflicts to be resolved and superceded, and that earlier experiences persist like geological layers unchanged by and unalloyed with later symbolic unconscious elaborations.

Rather than abandon developmental accounts, psychoanalytic theory needs to decenter its theory of development: later integrations should neither seamlessly subsume nor replace earlier positions but rather refigure them. This postulate would be analogous to Freud's idea of deferred action, *Nachtraeglichkeit* (see Laplanche and Pontalis 1973). According to this approach, later integrations would retain and refine earlier positions, changing their appearance yet not obliterating them, enabling a flexible oscillation between levels of experience. When integration is confused with reductive assimilation, development is rightly suspect as a high-priced form of impoverishment—as in the world of economic development, which has already wiped out whole species and landscapes, as well as the richness and beauty of different cultures. As Bataille elaborated in his critique of culture (1985), so we might say of identifications: heterogeneity is continually threatened by homogeneity, which tries to assimilate it.

If the critique of homogeneous gender development need not foreclose dynamic formulations about the development of gender identifications, it does demand suspicion of theories that assume gender development to be a simple trajectory toward heterosexual complementarity. Even when homosexuality is not directly pathologized, it is presented as a condition that needs to be explained, the object choice whose etiology requires continual and intense investigation. By contrast, as Chodorow points out (1992), heterosexual object choice is taken for granted, and it is seldom remarked that conventional heterosexuality does not require moving beyond the rigidly organized complementarities of gender polarity (see Chodorow 1992). As Kernberg (1991) has noted, insistence that the other be the heterosexual mirror image of the self, which includes intolerance of any other sexual elements, reflects a defense against envy, not an acceptance of difference. Of course, neither heterosexual nor homosexual relationships inherently guarantee a particular stance toward complementarity or sameness; either may succumb to fixity or play around with convention and previously fixed identities. It is apparent that psychoanalysis as an institution suffers from a significant cultural lag. It could learn something from the homosexual avant-garde's self-conscious and ironic play with gender conventions, which takes a deliberately critical stance toward identity, homo- or heterosexual, and thus has become the basis for theorizing, in Butler's (1990) term, subversions of identity.

Beyond the Oedipal

Such challenges to oedipal complementarity suggest the need for a reconsideration of the function and meaning of complementarity. What does it mean to posit the integration of the earlier overinclusive position with the later oedipal complementarity in the postoedipal phase? What would it mean to restore, at a higher level of differentiation, capacities that were excluded by oedipal rigidity? I have proposed that object love, which has sometimes been seen as opposed to, exclusive of, or replaced by identification, may also be seen as growing out of identificatory love. But what is the ongoing relationship between object love and identification, what becomes of identificatory love of the opposite sex later in life? Is this a simple proposition — that identification gives way to object love — a kind of reversal of the postulate that object love is replaced by identification in the ego? If not, how to conceptualize the way that identification remains part of love relationships throughout life?

These two sets of questions about the fate of identification and the integration of the overinclusive phase are related. My answer is that sustaining identificatory tendencies alongside object love creates a different kind of complementarity, and a different stance toward oppositional differences. It is possible to distinguish between two forms of complementarity. The earlier oedipal form is a simple opposition, constituted by splitting, projecting the unwanted elements into the other; in that form, what the other has is "nothing." The postoedipal form is constituted by sustaining the tension between contrasting elements so that they remain potentially available rather than forbidden and the oscillation between them can then be pleasurable rather than dangerous. Although the rigid form of sexual complementarity may actually utilize a well-elaborated representation of the other's role derived from previous identification, the self repudiates and is threatened by that role as an unwanted part.

As our culture is organized, the child must go through an oedipal period in which complementarity is accomplished by insisting on polarity: mutual exclusivity, black and white, male and female, can and cannot. Using Kohlberg's distinction between conventional and postconventional thinking, we could say that this oedipal polarizing corresponds to conventional thinking about difference, which is appropriate to this stage of children's moral and cognitive development. In Kohlberg's view, postconventional thinking does not develop until adolescence, and this would indeed be the period when we would expect the oedipal recrudescence to resolve with a more differentiated, flexible form of complementarity. In this vein Bassin (1991) has used the terms of genital theory to propose that the phallic phase, with its opposites *have* and *have not*, should give way in adolescence to a true genital phase, in which antithetical elements can be reunited. She proposes that the transcendence of the split unity of gender polarity is expressed through symbol formation, with its transitional bridging function. Unlike projective identification, symbolization reunites the antagonistic component tendencies (Freedman 1980, cited in Bassin 1994) — for instance, active and passive, phallic and containing.[7] Symbolization links rather than prohibits the gratification of both aims, expressing rather than masking the unconscious oscillation between them. The key to this symbolic

---

7. Bassin's use of the term "true genital" may be misleading insofar as it does not do justice to the pregenital aspects of preoedipal life, which should be reintegrated in the kind of synthesis of symbols she proposes. Samuels (1985) offers a Jungian view of symbols similar to hers, as reconciling opposites, and in so doing giving expression to a sense of awe and power. He cites a woman patient who dreamed of a pitchfork that had both feminine curves and phallic points, horrific nipples nonetheless connected to fertility. Similarly, an analyst reported to me a patient's dream in which a tampon seemed to represent something powerful, both phallic and a container for blood, which was both fertile and messy.

function is the recuperation of identification with the "missing half" of the complementarity: in symbolization "the familiar is found in the unfamiliar" (Freedman, cited in Bassin 1994).

The familiar can be found by "returning" to the overinclusive position, in which it was still possible to use the transitional space of communicative play to entertain wishes that reality denies — as when a three-year-old boy said to his mother, "I have a nipple on my penis, see, and the peepee comes out of the nipple." To pretend that the penis is a breast or that the anus is a vagina need not serve the denial of difference, as theories of perversion have stressed; in response to an earlier version of this essay I have been told of male patients for whom recovery of the fantasy of a vagina resolved unwanted sexual compulsion. Such fantasy play may also serve the symbolic bridging of difference acknowledged and enhance sexual empathy. Development thus requires not a unilinear trajectory away from the overinclusive position but the ability to return without losing the knowledge of difference. The more differentiated postconventional form of symbolic complementarity, which is no longer concrete and projective, requires access to the flexible identificatory capacities of preoedipal life.

This notion of recapturing overinclusive structures of identification and sublimating omnipotence is meant to incorporate the epistemological contribution of contemporary cultural theory, especially feminist theory, by decentering our notion of development and replacing the discourse of identity with the notion of plural identifications. At the same time, this perspective might offer a different kind of developmental and empirical support for contemporary feminist theorizing about gender. The postconventional relation to gender representations need not be seen as a utopian ideal; it is not merely drawn from theoretical speculation but is a material possibility, already visible in the interstices of the gender order. From the perspective of contemporary feminist theory, the problem is that there can be no position "outside" that order, outside the logic of gender, which constructs masculinity and femininity as binary opposites. If one posits some essential femininity that is not yet represented or defined, as Irigaray does, one tends merely to reinforce that logic (Rose 1982); thus Butler (1990) has argued, instead, for a notion of subversion. But what does subversion mean in psychoanalytic terms?

As I have tried to show, the postconventional complementarity, which recognizes the multiplicity and mutuality denied by the oedipal form, does not exist outside the gender system. It reworks its terms, disrupting its binary logic by breaking down and recombining opposites rather than by discovering something wholly different, unrepresented or unrepresentable. It subverts the oedipal complementarity through the leverage of its own negative tension — the impossibility of constituting a complementary system that can exclude all identification with otherness from the self. The postconventional complementarity relies on the psychic capacity to symbolically bridge split oppositions as well as on preoedipal overinclusiveness.

Psychoanalytic theory has, until recently, been unable to think beyond the oedipal level. This fixation is reflected in the prevailing theories that insist on heterosexual complementarity, that equate perversion with homosexuality and "genital whole object relations" with heterosexuality (see Chodorow 1992). The claim that the oedipal achievement of complementarity represents a renunciation of omnipotence and acceptance of limits — being only the one or the other — misses another dimension, the one that gives depth to the delineation of difference. It also serves to conceal the unconscious narcissism of oedipal chauvinism — being the "only thing" — for which Freud's theory of the girl as "little man" *manqué* was exemplary.

The oedipal move that adumbrates the position "I am the

one, you are the other," thereby creating the simple form of otherness, is organizing for both sexes. It is overtly hegemonic in the male form but covertly present in its opposite form, female contempt, as Dinnerstein (1976) pointed out. We may choose to speculate (see Chapter 3) that this oedipal move represents a simple reversal of the preoedipal, in which the mother seems to be everything, "generically human" (Chodorow 1979). In any case, the superordinate logic that underlies that move is one of mutual exclusivity, either/or, and it is instituted in the Oedipus complex. This mutual exclusivity is known to us, quite simply, as heterosexual complementarity. In this sense, the joining of heterosexual complementarity and binary opposition (Goldner 1991) in the oedipal moment constitutes "The" sexual Difference.

But the constitution of sexual differences in the multiple sense is not centered around one psychic complex. The reality of sexual differences is far more multifarious than the binary logic of mutual exclusivity allows. The psyche not only preserves unconsciously identifications that have been repudiated, it also expresses them unconsciously or consciously in sexual relations, between parents and children, and between lovers of whatever apparent object choices, imbuing them with far more complexity than this complementarity represents. Oedipal identifications, although pervasive at the level of gender ideals, do not seal off other development, other identifications, even though the theory represents them as doing so; they do not form a seamless, consistent, hegemonic structure that suppresses everything else in the psyche (Goldner 1991). They are, after all, only an organized and powerful set of fantasies.

But for the same reason, no absolute transcendence of the oedipal is possible. Delineating the binary logic of heterosexual complementarity is not equivalent to disavowing or getting rid of oedipal structures. It is no more possible to get rid of the omnipotent aspect of the oedipal position than to get rid of the preoedipal fantasy of omnipotence — or rather, it would be possible only in a wholly omnipotent world, one without loss, envy, and difference. But we can subvert the concealed omnipotence by exposing it, as well as by recognizing another realm of sexual freedom that reworks the oedipal terms. To be sure, this realm depends upon the other face of omnipotence: the overinclusive capacities to transcend reality by means of fantasy, which can be reintegrated in the sexual symbolic of the postoedipal phase.

The tension between the omnipotent wish for transcendence and the affirmation of limits has always found expression in the domains of aesthetic and erotic pleasure. Any effort to destabilize the fixed positions of gender complementarity depends upon the tension between limit and transgression — a limit those positions actually help to frame, a boundary in relation to which symbolic acts achieve their meaning. The knowledge of both core gender identification and the oedipal complementarity constitutes a background for the symbolic transgressions of fantasy, for the disruption of complementary oppositions and fixed identities.

The postoedipal complementarity also implies a less definite relation between object love and identification. Freud at one point described identification as the first emotional tie to the object, a way of being related to someone who is there, who is loved and not necessarily lost (1921). He seemingly gave up that idea in favor of identification as an internal process, a precipitate of abandoned, lost, and renounced objects (1923). This supercession, like other moves in oedipal theory, gave away as much as it gained. It probably functioned to turn attention away from identificatory love, the preoedipal period's most important legacy, which contributes to subsequent relationships of love and like. Again, the idea that object love and identification are mutually exclusive is an oedipal product, which neither adequately represents the unconscious relations of desire nor offers a particularly useful basis for bridging the gap between self and other. I see no reason that we cannot be more inclusive and recognize that identificatory love and object love can and do exist simultaneously. Why not see the movements from identification to object love, from object love to identification, as ongoing alternations throughout life? The unconscious can, as it does with other oppositions, switch and reverse them — the difficulty is to maintain them as tensions rather than breaking them down into split polarities. In postoedipal life object love may include aspects of identificatory love and vice versa. Like difference and sameness, object love and identificatory love constitute a tension that should not be seen as requiring resolution.

Nor are the sides precisely what they have appeared to be within the binary logic of gender complementarity. In that logic of the One and the Other, there is no place for the Both or the Many. If sex and gender as we know them are oriented to the pull of opposing poles, then these poles are not masculinity and femininity. Rather, gender dimorphism itself represents only one pole — its other pole is the polymorphism of all individuals.

3 / The Omnipotent Mother: A Psychoanalytic Study of Fantasy and Reality

Karen Horney (1932) began her classic essay "The Dread of Woman" with Schiller's poem about "The Diver" whose search for a woman doomed him to the perils of the engulfing deep. Horney suggests that man's longing for woman is always coupled with "the dread that through her he might die and be undone." This fear may be concealed either by contempt or by adoration: contempt repairs the injury to masculine self-esteem, whereas adoration covers dread with awe and mystery. Speculating on the origin of these feelings, Horney declares, "If the grown man continues to regard woman as a great mystery, in whom is a secret he cannot divine, this feeling of his can only relate ultimately to one thing in her: the mystery of motherhood" (p. 135). Modern disenchantment has no doubt worked to diminish the mystique surrounding procreation and motherhood. But the eclipse of this immediate sense of mystery has scarcely alleviated the dread of maternal power; it has only ban-

An earlier version of this essay appeared in *Representations of Motherhood*, ed. D. Bassin, M. Honey, and M. Kaplan (New Haven: Yale University Press, 1994), 129–146. Used by permission.

ished it to the darkness beyond the portals of enlightenment. There it remains alive, in the unconscious if you will, where it still serves diverse — divers — fantastic purposes.

In a notable parallel to Horney's remarks, Freud referred to Schiller's diver when he discussed the origins of religious feeling in *Civilization and Its Discontents*. Freud's reflections on his own lack of experience with the oceanic feeling led him to this association: "I am moved to exclaim, in the words of Schiller's diver: 'He may rejoice, who breathes in the roseate light'" (1930, p. 73). Reading these lines we may find a submerged meaning in his analysis of religion. Where Freud recognizes in religion the earliest wish to be rescued by the father from primary helplessness, we may discern in that vision of helplessness a fear of the maternal depths. The projection of an all-powerful father emerges from that fear of the oceanic oneness, an antidote to helplessness at the hands of a dreaded maternal power.

In its manifest form, the notion that the child begins in helpless dependency upon a mother from whom he must separate has guided psychoanalytic thinking ever since Freud's formulations. This notion has repeatedly led to the proposition that men had to denigrate or dominate women to compensate for their dependency upon and envy of the mother, who can give birth and nurture the young. Because it is necessary for men to separate from mother and give up their original identification with her, the pull to her is felt as a threat to their independent identity (Stoller 1975).[1] This argument underlies the most common psychoanalytic explanations for male dominance; it has been elaborated by psychoanalysts sympathetic to

1. A prominent exposition of this interpretation is Stoller's *Perversion* (1975). Earlier versions can be found in Otto Rank's work, cited by Herbert Marcuse in *Eros and Civilization* (1962). Marcuse took a positive view of regression to maternal oneness, as did N. O. Brown in *Life Against Death* (1959), but this view continued to promulgate the basic bifurcation in which the father represents the reality principle, the mother pleasure.

feminism like Robert Stoller (1975) and by the feminist theorist Dorothy Dinnerstein (1976).

In a related argument, Chasseguet-Smirgel (1976) challenged Freud's theory of phallic monism, the notion that the vagina was unknown to children. She contended that the oedipal boy's conscious image of the little girl as inferior and lacking (which Horney had pinpointed as the psychic correlate of Freud's theory) is a reversal of the boy's unconscious image of the mother as powerful and overwhelming. If, as the theory contends, children know consciously only of the penis, this stance is actually an effort to repair a narcissistic wound, the sense of helplessness and dependency on the omnipotent mother, whose vagina is too large. This primary helplessness later takes the form of the oedipal realization that one is too small to satisfy or complete mother. The original threat is not castration by the father but narcissistic injury in relation to the mother. Unavoidably, the admired and powerful phallic father actually saves the child from helplessness at the hands of the mother. The "natural scorn" for women that Freud often noted is an effect of the transfer of power to the father, which at once conceals and assuages fear of the mother. But Chasseguet-Smirgel, like a wide range of psychoanalytic thinkers before her — Fromm and Lacan, to suggest the extremes — accepts the transfer of power to the father as the only means by which the child can free him- or herself from helpless subjection to the omnipotent mother and enter the reality of the wider world.

Dinnerstein, in a significant departure from this position, regarded this scheme of paternal rescue from early dependency on the omnipotent mother as inherently problematic. She sees the escape from unfreedom by embracing paternal authority not as necessary but rather as part of a constellation that constitutes our cultural sickness. If the infant projects omnipotence upon the first person who cares for her or him, Dinnerstein believes that this projection can be defused only by giving men an equal role in nurturing children in infancy. Were men also to embody the dangerous, enchanting thrall of early intimacy, we could no longer split off all the envy, greed, dread, and rage and apply it to women. Dinnerstein's logic presumes that there is no structure of gender difference apart from parenting roles, a convenient but untenable solution because it leaves out the structure of heterosexuality and its cultural representation. Further, Dinnerstein's conclusion is that the wish for omnipotence and its projection onto more powerful others are inevitable reactions to dependency for which there is no antidote.

Chodorow, though often identified with Dinnerstein, actually criticizes Dinnerstein for her assumption that the fantasy of maternal omnipotence springs from the real dependence on the mother and for equating woman with mother (Chodorow and Contratto 1982). Chodorow (1979) ascribes to the child's psyche an ability to recognize the mother's subjectivity, to see her as like subject and not just as needed object. Hence there is a psychic force of differentiation that might serve to counterbalance omnipotence. While Dinnerstein's postulate of female mothering as an original universal cause of human malaise seems too sweeping, indeed, omnipotent, Chodorow's solution too quickly forecloses an elaboration of omnipotence and therefore an understanding of how it might be modified. She and Contratto suggest (Chodorow and Contratto 1982) that omnipotent tendencies can be countered by secondary process, conscious determination, and rational knowledge of consequences. But if children are endowed with, among other capacities, the ability to recognize the mother's subjectivity, one has to ask why this capacity consistently loses out.

Irigaray, reflecting on these issues, links the denial of maternal dependency to the failure of representation that erases the mother. In a more dramatic argument, she states that in Orestes' murder of Clytemnestra the polis was founded on matricide, hence on the sacrifice of the first body on which we depend, a body that "has become a devouring monster as an inverted effect of the blind consumption of the mother" (1991, p. 40). It is this blindness, the inability to symbolically represent that first relation and the separation from it, that makes of woman a dangerous hole into which the individual may disappear. The question of where, precisely, this inversion occurs and what prevents the representation of the mother is thus linked to the problem of omnipotence. We might consider Chodorow's (1979) proposal that the repudiation of the mother in the oedipal phase constitutes a crucial moment (see also Benjamin 1988) in which the male turns the table on the female so that the reversal of power relations becomes enmeshed with male cultural hegemony. Leaving aside the question of the original, founding crime, it is necessary to analyze how the deeply rooted cultural bifurcation of all experience under the poles of heterosexually organized gender attenuates recognition of the mother's subjectivity and perpetuates the fantasy of omnipotence. I intend to show how this works by unpacking the relationship between reality and fantasy in the context of the establishment of gender.

I begin with a deliberately double-sided perspective to encompass the duality of psychic life, both the fantasy of maternal omnipotence and the capacity to recognize the mother as another subject. A mode of intersubjective reality — that is, a relationship between two or more different subjects sharing certain feelings or perceptions — coexists with a mode of fantasy as the unshared property of an isolated subject. The capacity to recognize the mother as another subject and the fantasy of maternal omnipotence are aligned with this duality. Ideally these distinct psychic tendencies of our psychic organization constitute a tension rather than, as has often been supposed, a contradiction, an "either-or." It would be naive to imagine that we could cleanse the psyche of dangerous fantasies or that such a purge would not carry off everything we value as well. But we might imagine a way to balance the fantastic register, in which self and objects can be omnipotent, with the intersubjective register, in which we recognize, feel, and symbolically represent the subjectivity of real others. It is the breakdown of the tension between these two modes, not the existence of fantasy (omnipotence) per se, that prevents the recognition of other subjects.

This breakdown is best illustrated by Horney's remarks on man's dread of woman: " 'It is not,' He says, 'that I dread her; it is that *she* herself *is* malignant, capable of any crime, a beast of prey, a vampire, a witch, insatiable in her desires. *She is* the very personification of what is sinister.' " This usage — *She is* — is an important key to the whole matter. The symbolic equation (Segal 1957) signifies a collapse of reality and fantasy, as when analysand says to analyst, "I know this feeling I have about you has to do with my mother, but unfortunately I've ended up with you, who really are just like her." All that is bad and dreaded is projected onto the other, and all the anxiety is seen as the product of external attack rather than one's own subjective state. The problem, then, is not simply that male children disidentify with and then repudiate the mother. It is also that this repudiation involves the psyche in those projective processes — "she *is* . . . " — that intensify the fear of the other's omnipotence as well as the need to retaliate by asserting one's own omnipotence.

The process of recognition, to some degree, breaks up these projective processes and modifies omnipotence. I have discussed in Chapter 1 the way in which we have come to understand early development as a process that involves mutual recognition, but we should briefly address the idea of oneness or perfection. Infancy theorists (D. Stern 1985; Beebe and Lachmann 1988) have argued that even at four months an attuned mother is not undifferentiated, does not create the illusion of perfect oneness. Indeed, even in those interactions that appear harmonious, Beebe and Lachmann (1994) have contended, such a mother matches her baby only part of the time — more than midrange responsiveness usually constitutes not harmony but control. In her play she stimulates an incipient recognition of otherness, difference, and discrepancy. The infant, in turn, relishes the excitement that a brush with otherness brings. Later, at about nine months, the infant begins to be aware of the fact that, as Daniel Stern (1985) described it, separate minds can share similar states (see Chapter 1). The child is able to realize that another shares his or her intention or excitement, which is conveyed by translating the action into a different modality, not by direct imitation. The metaphor of the mirror is therefore not appropriate to early mothering: mirror imitation is less satisfying than complex interaction. What *feels* perfect never *is* perfect.

The original psychoanalytic theory or ideal of a mother who offers a perfect oceanic symbiosis might be seen as an extremely idealized and oversimplified view of the infant's experience. This image exemplifies the Freudian idea of *Nachtraeglichkeit* or deferred action (see Laplanche and Pontalis, 1973), a subsequent reworking of early experience. It is a reading backward through the lens of loss, the encounter with which generates the wish for omnipotence and the projection of the longing for symbiotic oneness upon the mother. Psychoanalytic theory has adduced this originary oneness to explain the fear of regression that is the basis of the dread of mother and of woman. How did the trope of oneness come to inform the whole theory of infancy? If men and women both project the dangerous longing for a return to amniotic life onto the mother, is this not itself a symptom of a breakdown in tension between fantasy and reality?

Psychoanalytic theory has thus been largely unable to conceptualize the mother as a separate subject, to see the mother-child relationship from the viewpoint of both subjects. While showing the infant's capacity for recognition, the new perspective on infant perception of the mother goes only part way toward an intersubjective view. In any case, this perspective should not be taken just as a product of adhering to empirical observation; to assume that would be naive. The search for new methodologies, the awareness of the implausibility of old theories of an autistic withdrawn infant, the focus on mutuality, all can be seen as a result of new discursive systems. Even if, as in this case, scientific development seems to reflect and reinforce changes in the ideology of motherhood and women's status, we may wish to take some distance from a paradigm that grants the mother so much responsibility and so little concern for the conditions of her own subjectivity. What we may safely derive from this perspective is that the mere fact of helpless dependency in infancy does not explain man's infantile stance in his fantasy of the mother. We discover, rather, that certain theoretical assumptions about dependency serve to reencode the lost mother as a dangerous other. Once our representation of the psyche includes intersubjectivity — a "counterforce" to omnipotence — it is possible to ask what allows us to tolerate dependency. How does an appreciation of shared reality open up a space for fantasy that is less dangerous?

I have suggested that mental omnipotence is a complex intrapsychic condition, not an immediate, originary state.[2] It

---

2. That is, we can postulate a state in which the limits of reality are not known and the other is experienced as "there" without awareness of an opposing center of intentionality. In it, power is not yet constructed as the opposite of powerlessness.

probably begins in the first crisis of recognizing the other, the first conscious encounter with the mother's independence, during the separation-individuation phase in the second year of life. The infant's grandiose aspirations now conflict with the perceived reality of her limitations and dependency. When the child becomes aware that reality will not always bend to her will, a "struggle to the death for recognition" may ensue. It is no accident that Mahler's observational studies of this period, which she called rapprochement, focused on mother's leaving (Mahler, Pine, and Bergman 1975), for mother's departure (to work, to go out) confronts the child with mother's independent aims, a point usually ignored. It also confronts the mother with the problem of her own separate existence. This is not just a matter of separation anxiety, as it is frequently portrayed, but of recognition — recognize my will, do as I want, stay here! For the mother, of course, this demanding child is a disillusionment: *her* fantasy of the perfect child would want what she wants. She must also relinquish her fantasy that she can be perfect and provide a perfect world for her child, a blow to her narcissism — she must accept that injuring the child's sense of complete control over her is a step on the child's road to recognition. In contrast to the Mahlerian ego psychology, I emphasize that the mother is facilitating more than frustration tolerance or object constancy: she is helping her child to get a first glimmer of the momentous idea that mother is a person in her own right.

This formulation emphasizes the mother's contribution to

But this is not the state we have experiential knowledge of and refer to as omnipotence. Omnipotence is the reactive effort to recreate that presumed state, as if power could be known before the knowledge of powerlessness and difference, which is actually the condition of power. This reconstruction creates omnipotence, which can then be understood as defensive denial, not simple ignorance, of the other's independence. Omnipotence holds the same place as primary narcissism in our theory, and Sheperdson (1993) has identified a similar defensive operation, theorizing primary narcissism as mythical, "the retroactively reconstructed unity that has been lost."

the early power struggles and so might seem to imply that she bears sole responsibility for her own recognition by the child. I shall revise this picture later, taking up the structural issues that more deeply affect the outcome of maternal recognition. But in order to clarify the processes for and against omnipotence, let us consider the conventional psychoanalytic picture of the mother who passes on her own solutions to the dilemma of omnipotence. When the mother is unable to set a clear boundary for the child and to respect the child's intentions and desire, she is likely to appear not as a person but as an all-powerful figure, either omnipotently controlling or engulfingly weak. What we are tracking is how the child comes to have a sense of shared reality. The point here is not to dismiss fantasy, play, or the narcissism of Her or His Majesty, the baby, but to acknowledge the necessity of struggle. Ideally, as I stated earlier, the paradox of recognition is not resolved but remains as a tension between self-assertion and recognition.

The process that I want to elucidate here allows a shift in psychic balance so that the confrontation with the other can result in a greater appreciation of the other's independent subjectivity. We want to know what allows a person to tolerate conflict without withdrawing from a sense of mutuality, and what, in contrast, reinforces the sense of omnipotence. Winnicott, as I discussed in Chapter 1, formulated the idea that in the course of development we do a rather paradoxical thing: we try to destroy the other person in order to discover that they survive. The paradox is that only by asserting omnipotence may we discover the other as an outside center of experience. By destroying the other, not literally but in fantasy, by absolutely asserting the self and negating the other's separateness in our minds, we discover that the other is outside our mental powers. In a sense, the other stands for the implacable outside reality — but not too implacable, since this process works only if the other continues to be an effective, responsive, and nonthreatening presence.

Winnicott's concept can be seen as a paradigm for the ongoing oscillations between omnipotence and recognition throughout life rather than as a strictly sequential notion, in which the infant begins in omnipotence and moves out toward reality in a unilinear fashion. Understood in this way, the alternation of destruction and survival augments a vision in which fantasy and reality can be more or less differentiated, rather than canceling out each other. We do not suppress our fantasy that the other could perfectly meet our wishes, but we acknowledge it as fantasy, tolerate its distance from reality. The problem that often occurs in the process of differentiation is that if the other retaliates or caves in and withdraws, we don't really experience the other as outside us; instead of surviving and becoming real, she or he is subsumed by (seems to *be*) our persecutory fantasy. A power struggle is inaugurated, and the outcome is a reversible cycle of doer and done to. If the mother does not survive, a pattern is established in which there is no real other subject, no real feeling for the other. Let us imagine a mother who gives in to the child and never leaves. The child feels she or he has succeeded in controlling Mother, and this means "Now Mommy is still my fantasy, Mommy is also afraid, and I can never leave Mommy without great anxiety, either." Thus, even as the child loses contact with the real independent mother, the omnipotent fantasy mother fills the space. Now the child is no longer able to encompass the feeling "I am full of anxiety" but rather feels Mother must remain literally there to solve his problem. Otherwise, he experiences his fear and anger as if in reaction to a real, outside danger. Fantasy and reality are not distinct. If, alternately, Mother leaves and returns, followed by a happy reunion, the child feels that the danger — the projection of his own anger onto Mother — was not real.

To extend the implications of Winnicott's analysis, when aggression is not worked through in this way, it continues to fuel fantasies of revenge and retaliation, attributed to both self and other. The whole experience is removed from the domain of intersubjective reality and becomes the exclusive domain of unconscious fantasy, positioned not as a feeling we can own but as a projection onto the frightening, dreaded object. All inter-subjective experience is elaborated in fantasy, as I have said, but when the other does not survive and aggression is not dissi-pated, experience becomes almost exclusively fantastic. The broader issue is thus not the danger of fantasies per se but a loss of balance whereby fantasies of frightening objects overshadow all psychic experience.

The negotiation of paradox with the other (see Pizer 1992) allows the infant's original fascination with and love for what is outside, the appreciation of what is different and challenging, to inform more complex social relationships. Thus psychic separa-tion encompasses more than internalization of the object in order to leave it, and the aggression that often accompanies separation can be creatively sublimated rather than merely de-fensive. The process of negotiating conflict and establishing a shared reality — in which one has a sense of agency and impact — helps to rework experiences of anger and abandonment.

In this vein I referred in Chapter 1 to First's (1988) observa-tions on the way in which mother's leaving for work was repre-sented by two-year-old children. The children's symbolic play evolved from an aggressive, retaliatory reaction to an identifica-tion with the leaving mother who misses the child. In the initial position the child reverses roles and insists that the mother play the child, gleefully ordering her to cry. But soon the glee at reversing the inflicted suffering is mixed with and transformed by identification with the mother's subjective experience of missing her child. From this realization of shared mourning the child can also conclude, "I know that you could wish to have your own life as I wish to have mine." In the transition from a retaliatory world of control to a world of mutual understanding, the child gets to recognize that the leaving mother is not only separate but a center of subjective experience not unlike the child's.

Let me sum up the problem of holding onto both shared reality and omnipotent fantasy. The initial response to the discovery of the difference between my will and your will is a breakdown of recognition between self and other: I insist on my way, I refuse to recognize you, I try to coerce you. I therefore experience your refusal as a reversal: you are coercing me. This breakdown can be repaired only by the reciprocal identification, expressed in communicative play, that gives the relief and pleasure of contacting the other mind. Along the way, the initial effort at retaliatory reversal may be a kind of empowerment: "I can do to you what you do to me." A necessary step, the ability to play with omnipotence fantasies, gives a taste of freedom and tests survival. Survival is followed by the emotional identification with the other's position, an identification that includes the ability to reflexively articulate the difference. This simultaneous advance in symbolic identification and differentiation permits the child to work through complementarity to a new position of reflexivity so that he or she, as First says, is able to share feelings without fearing that these are simply the other's feelings.

There is now a space between the mother and child that symbolically contains negative feelings such that they need not be projected onto the object ("she is dreadful") or turned back upon the self ("I am destructive"). The relationship can alternate between the complementarity of doer and done to and the symmetry of reciprocal identification. The unreflexive complementary structure dictates a reversible relationship, which allows one to switch roles but not to alter them or hold them simultaneously: power is not dissolved but kept moving, like a hot potato, from one partner to the other; domination can be reversed but not undone.

When the tension between complementarity and mutuality breaks down — individually or culturally — the absence of a real other creates a kind of paranoid free fall. The cycle of destroying the reality of the other and filling the void with the fantasy of a feared and denigrated object, one who must be controlled for fear of retaliation, characterizes all relations of domination. Again, the problem is the positioning of the fantasy. My contention regarding sadomasochistic fantasies is that domination follows not from the provisional enjoyment of complementary power fantasies but from the fixity of complementary positions; domination follows from the inability to sustain the tension between the two sides, which is first the result and later the condition of the other's survival.

The paradox of recognition is not solved once and for all but remains an organizing issue throughout life, becoming intense with each fresh struggle for independence, each confrontation with difference. If omnipotence fantasies are ubiquitous and complementarity persists, this is not the result of a one-shot maternal failure. Nor is it necessary that the fantasy of maternal omnipotence be dispelled, only that it be modified by the existence of another dimension — that of intersubjectivity. As in the toddler's discovery of identification with the leaving mother, intersubjectivity and symbolization evolve through the space of communicative interaction and fantasy play in the dyad. Lacking this space, the projective power of the fantasy becomes too virulent: "She *is* that thing I feel" (see Ogden 1986). Symptomatic, again, is the formulation of the symbolic equation, a function prior to symbolization, in which the symbol does not stand for the thing, it *is* that thing (Segal 1957). In the symbolic equation (She *is* that thing) the verb "to be" closes space opened by the verbs "seem" or "feel" — by the action of play and just-pretend.

The intersubjective space — Winnicott's potential space (1969b) — between mother and child establishes the distinction between the symbol and the symbolized. As Ogden (1986) has contended, the subject who can begin to make this distinction has access to a triangular field — symbol, symbolized, and the interpreting subject. The space between self and other facilitates the distinction, let us say, between the real mother and the symbolic mother. This notion of the evolution of space in the early maternal dyad (see Trevarthen 1980) need not be attributed to the intervention of a "third term," as Lacan argued; rather, it reflects the evolving capacity of communicative interaction to digest and transform affect and create self-other awareness. Eigen (1981) proposes that in Winnicott's thinking self-other awareness itself forms the core of "symbolizing experiencing," a preverbal alternative to Lacan's linguistic notion of the symbolic.[3]

What happens to close that intersubjective space whose symbolic processes counter omnipotence? At this point an explanation is required that goes beyond the mother's response to her child, beyond the individual level. Heretofore this question did not constitute a problem for psychoanalytic theory, which, with few exceptions, did not try to conceptualize an alternative to the complementarity of subject-object relations. Understanding the roots of domination to lie in narcissism, the theory

3. By the same logic, this conception of the mother-child dyad is an alternative to the Lacanian notion of a "primordially split subject," whose existence requires postulating an "originally lost object" (J. Mitchell 1982). Rather, the potential space emerges through sequencing of lost and found, through digestion of loss and recovery, through disruption and repair (Tronick 1989; Beebe and Lachmann, 1994). The transitional space with the object who is neither absolutely lost nor present allows symbolic experience to take shape. An absolute loss would actually lead to a traumatic foreclosure of the symbolic, not to its emergence.

envisioned overcoming narcissism only through the oedipal structure of subordination to paternal authority, usually conceived as a kind of universal principle or law (see, for example, Chasseguet-Smirgel 1985). The theory took for granted the impossibility of achieving recognition within the dyad; it assumed that two subjects alone could never confront each other without merging, one being subordinated and assimilated by the other; and it gave the father the role of bringing the child into reality and creating the triangular field. Thus Juliette Mitchell, summing up a position taken by many Lacanian feminists, wrote, "To date, the father stands in the position of the third term that must break the asocial dyadic unity of mother and child. We can see that this term will always need to be represented by something or someone" (1982, p. 23).

The issue is not the idea that only the father can represent the third term, a concrete, literal notion that all feminists might question (Rose 1982). Rather, the issue is whether we believe that an external force must "break" the dyad, whether we even think that the dyad is "asocial" or a "unity." We might instead view this representation of a third term as an effect generated by the symbolic space within a social, differentiated maternal dyad. If the identification of the symbolic function with the agency of the father or third person were itself a symbolic effect, it would be the collapse into symbolic equation that we would want to investigate. Let us speculate that this collapse could be the result of foreclosing the negotiation of recognition with the mother, of transferring her omnipotence rather than dissolving it. The distinction between symbol and thing would then disappear, and the father's function would appear to *be* the engendering of difference, not merely to stand for it. And so a rendition of the oedipal solution would emerge, in which paternal power appears to be a necessity of culture (J. Mitchell 1974); the displacement of mother's power onto father would be posed as the way out of omnipotence rather than the effect of it.

Yet this "solution" actually constructs the undifferentiated maternal ideal it purports to cure. Rather than negotiating with mother's power to abandon or control the child, the struggle around separation and recognition is split off from the maternal figure. The anger and loss in relation to her are not felt and worked through; instead, power and aggression are simply redirected onto a rival father (Sprengnether 1995).[4] The omnipotence once attributed to her is revived in the fantasy of paternal rescue — as in Freud's view of religion. In the oedipal solution the mother is at once idealized as unattainable object of goodness and repudiated as possible subject; the "other woman" becomes the denigrated but tempting sexual object, frequently the target of the split-off aggression that was felt toward the controlling, powerful mother. This splitting bars the way to the representation of women's sexual subjectivity and denies the mother's oedipal sexuality. The oedipal complementarity negates the mother's subjectivity by locating her in what Kristeva (1986) has termed the fantasy of a "lost territory." This fantasy is, in effect, less about the maternal relationship than about "the idealization of primary narcissism" (Kristeva 1986, p. 161; discussed in Sheperdson 1993).

---

4. Sprengnether's analysis of Freud's courtship letters (1995) makes a compelling case for the way in which Freud's own maternal idealization, his difficulty in acknowledging loss in relation to his mother, and his reiterated belief in a mother's unambivalent love of the firstborn son contributed to his formulation of the Oedipus complex. In his self-analysis, from which his theory derives, Freud's aggression is turned toward the father, as is, in the wake of his father's death, the consciousness of loss. Sprengnether contends that unacknowledged grief and mourning for the mother, with whom there can be no struggle, lead to a series of displacements, culminating in the centrality of aggression (see also Sprengnether 1990). A close reading of *Beyond the Pleasure Principle* shows how aggression and death (the final separation) come to hold the place of loss in his theory.

But this relocation of the mother and the denial of her sexuality have likewise been reinforced by the feminist counter-move, which has excluded the oedipal moment from theorizing about the mother. This exclusion, with its avoidance of the problem of sexual difference, has been forcefully challenged by the Lacanian feminist positions (see J. Mitchell 1982; Rose 1982, 1986; Ragland-Sullivan 1986). That challenge reinforces my sense that, however questionable the oedipal model's retroactive legitimation of patriarchy may be, it is necessary to analyze the preoedipal mother's transformation as it is filtered through the heterosexual, oedipal structure. In fact, to bypass oedipal history, as if one could excavate the utopian prehistory of the mother like that of an earlier civilization, is to create an imaginary "realm of the senses, outside of all history and form" — a danger Rose (1986) believes is inherent in Kristeva's account of the maternal semiotic. Any effort to reverse direction, roll back the frames, and extract a purely presymbolic body will subscribe, albeit in defiant opposition, to the same oedipal construction. The point is therefore not to counter repudiation with rescue — to imagine a mother free of, prior to, the oedipal structure — but to "see through" that structure like a translucent layer. We may then demystify the ostensibly undifferentiated perfection — omnipotence as oneness — of the preoedipal maternal dyad as an idealized appearance produced by the Oedipal discourse. This demystification is of utmost importance, for, as Kristeva (1981) declared, "If the archetype of the belief in a good and pure substance, that of utopias, is the belief in the omnipotence of an archaic, full, total englobing mother with no frustration, no separation, no break-producing symbolism (with no castration, in other words)" then it is possible to "defuse the violences" endemic to utopianism only by challenging the "myth of the archaic mother" (p. 32).

How does one challenge such a myth? Not by defending

the paternal function and heterosexuality as Kristeva does, but, as I have suggested, by grasping the real ambivalence of the maternal relation, and thus of the paternal relation as well. The effort to demystify the maternal relationship reveals its double-sidedness: a complex struggle of destruction and recognition already well under way in the preoedipal dyad. But we also require an analysis of how the oedipal drama, with its valorization of the paternal, occludes and retroactively refigures the maternal, reducing it to that archaic, idealized phantasm that haunts us. To this end, it may be illuminating to examine more closely the process Freud (1937) called the repudiation of femininity.

The oedipal constellation is characterized by the polarization of object love and identification — the prohibition on having and being the same object. This prohibition prevents the boy from using the most common psychic method of dealing with loss and separation — trying to "be" the lost object, the mother. As a result, the mother threatens to become omnipotent once again; she appears, as Dinnerstein (1976) eloquently described, more monster than human sexual subject, more It than I, "that thing I dread." Of course, the oedipal boy and girl suffer similar disappointment of the deep longing for and bitter exclusion from the object of desire. But when being the object and having the object become mutually exclusive, identification is foreclosed, and the result is a more frightening loss; this stimulates a more dangerous representation of the maternal sexual object as dreaded, engulfing, overwhelming, and tantalizing. Loss and separation now may intensify rather than dissolve omnipotence, which resounds in the empty psychic space of fantasy. At this level, the loved object has been destroyed and retaliation or death — the ultimate withdrawal and separation — is fantasized. Fear of death and the fantasy of heroically fighting a personified Death or death-dealing figures of mythology

(Medusa, for instance) are common preoccupations of oedipal boys.

Repudiation also effectively interrupts the struggle with the mother for recognition, which might otherwise reaffirm her survival as well as allow the mutual identification typical of the oedipal rivalry. It arrests the working through of complementarity to the point at which the reversal of omnipotence can give way to identification with the mother's nurturant and containing activity. (Typical gender differences in adopting the complementary role can be seen in latency. For instance, an older child is asked to entertain a younger one: the boy takes the toddler's toy and operates it for him or her; the girl says to the little one, "Show me how you do that." Both a boy and a girl notice that mother is tired and dispirited: the girl suggests that mother watch the television news, which she knows mother likes; the boy suggests mother listen to his new rock 'n' roll tape.) The representation of the mother-child relationship is retroactively reorganized as a dual unity, supplanting the recent past of relative differentiation with the distant past of babyhood, which is either disdained or inaccessible. The boy now refers to all babies as "she" and perceives maternal activity to be unmasculine. The repudiation of the position of the baby, as well as of the mother's empathy for the baby, leaves the internal baby lonely, debased, and uncontained.

Coupled with the loss of identification, the oedipal experience of sexuality makes of the tantalizing mother a disturbing and dangerous figure, who could be as ferocious as the boy's unsatisfied desire, a toothy or engulfing vagina. In defense against both overstimulation and abandonment, the boy effects another reversal: maternal sexual activity is appropriated to the masculine, and infantile passivity is attributed to the mother, the feminine sexual object. This oedipal reversal of active and passive has also uncritically entered psychoanalytic theory, in much the same way that, as Horney showed, Freud's theory of female sexuality corresponded to the thinking of the oedipal boy. Or, as Chasseguet-Smirgel (1976) added, the boy's oedipal defense against the unconsciously overwhelming mother takes the form of the idea that only the male genital is known to children (phallic monism). A parallel to this correspondence of theory and oedipal convictions has been revealed by Christiansen's (1993) deconstruction of Freud's early writings on hysteria and defense. His reading shows how Freud implicitly explains that masculine activity originates in the defensive reversal of passivity, the helpless subjection to overwhelming stimulation. It is this very helplessness in the face of overstimulation from which the mother's activity—nurturing and containing—originally protected the child.

Thus Freud's writings frequently relied on references to both maternal activity and feminine passivity, a paradox of which he was himself aware (e.g., Freud 1933). It would seem that the equations masculine = active, feminine = passive, which Freud alternately expounded and criticized, reflect another element of the defensive reversal of complementarity, whereby the boy says to the mother, "You are now the helpless baby, which I no longer am." The vulnerable dependency of the baby is projected onto the mother, who must accordingly hold the position of both feminine passivity and maternal activity.

The aspect of feminine passivity, however, can be seen to devolve from mother onto the figure of the daughter. One might speculate that the oedipal passivity that Freud expected the girl to adopt in her relation to the father is shaped by the oedipal boy's construction. Indeed, we might think that the oedipal reversal constructs the feminine at the same moment that it repudiates it. Mediated through the culture, the man (still feeling like the oedipal boy) locates his daughter/sexual object in the place he has renounced: "Yes sir, she's my baby."

This "feminine" representation, the transmuting of his own position of dependency and powerlessness, now becomes the defining term for woman sexual object, as wife or daughter—at times (as in the helpless waif) portrayed so like his own boyish appearance as to disclose the resemblance with his younger self that she personifies.[5] The assumption (willing or defiant) of this "feminine" position is theorized as the girl's oedipal task, the oft-repeated yet never fully explicable "switch" from active love of the mother to being the father's complementary object. The internal motive for the girl's taking up a position of father love may not, however, be equivalent to an identification with passivity; rather, it may be an offshoot of her complex effort to identify with his younger self as boy, as well as to identify with her potent and fertile mother.

Crucial to this power reversal, and to the simultaneous construction of activity and passivity, is the father's representation of the opposite term to femininity, the active masculine ideal. The boy effects the transfer of the mother's envied power onto father and then identifies with it, rather than directly appropriating maternal activity as a form of power and taking the mother as a rival. In this way, often enough, bits of maternal identification may enter through the back door as paternal protectiveness toward women and children; or, when contemporary fathers lift the cover of repudiation and openly express the wish for maternal activity, identifications can be recuperated—sometimes directly, sometimes obliquely, in the form of rivalry and envy. On the other hand, if the mother's powerlessness and lack of subjectivity dominate the boy's perception, he turns to

5. This unconscious fantasy construction of feminine sexuality as the position of baby/daughter obviously contributes to acceptance, if not the enactment, of sexual abuse. The dread/rejection in relation to the mother's active sexuality is coupled with the displacement onto the daughter of a reversed sexuality; she now becomes the passive victim of stimulation.

homoerotic ideal love of the father to escape the emptiness of her engulfing weakness.

Yet another element of reversal, as I have mentioned, is reflected in the theory of phallic monism: the repudiation of femininity in the genital stance. A seldom recognized aspect of the boy's denial of the vagina is that it represents a shift from one form of omnipotence wish to another. The preoedipal child's omnipotence takes the form of "overinclusiveness" (Fast 1984), of identifying bisexually with both sexes (Fast 1990). The child in the preoedipal phase wishes to be "everything," to incorporate polymorphously the organs and abilities of both sexes. It is only later that the oedipal child realizes that anatomical genders are mutually exclusive, that she or he cannot be everything and so defensively denies the value of the other organs. Children of both sexes insist that what they have is "the only thing" (Mayer 1985). The scornful denial of feminine organs (Chasseguet-Smirgel 1976) represents more than a compensation for the oedipal boy's narcissistic injury, for his realization that he is too small to satisfy mother. The contempt for mother's bodily amplitude and fertility also expresses the oedipal boy's move to deal with envy of what he has loved and with painful difference. As Irigaray (1985) shows, Freud's theory embodies this move, which, far from confronting sexual difference, acknowledges only one sex, only the masculine representation and the feminine lack. Traditional oedipal theorizing states that the boy realizes he cannot have mother, accepts the limit father sets, and so gives up omnipotent control over the primary object. It fails to realize that omnipotence is restored when that which he gives up is turned into "nothing" and the father with his phallus is now endowed with "everything."[6]

6. Lacan, for whom the phallus plays the role of privileged signifier, inadvertently provided an excellent illustration of the oedipal move from loss of the

Thus, in the polarized constellation of heterosexual identity, the recognition of mother's independent desire and subjectivity is blocked by unprocessed feelings of envy and fear of maternal sexuality, overstimulation, and abandonment. Although the oedipal achievement of complementarity is supposed by the theory to represent mature acceptance of difference and limits — being only the one or the other — it actually harbors the unconscious narcissistic omnipotence of being "the one and only." The principal reaction to giving up identification with the opposite sex or, shall we say, to the discovery of exclusive difference in the oedipal phase is a reassertion of omnipotence in a new form, chauvinism based on repudiation: "I must be the One, not the Other." Once we have recognized the finesse in the oedipal maneuver, the point is not to imagine a position completely independent of oedipal complementarity, which is no more possible than to eliminate all omnipotence. The point is rather to expose it and the myths to which it gives rise. To challenge the concealed omnipotence in the heterosexual structure — its principle of exclusivity and invidious comparison — is not to abrogate difference or to institute defensive notions of being everything. It is, rather, to integrate the preoedipal identifications of boys with mother and of girls with father as identifications with difference, which sufficiently modify the sense of loss, envy, and concomitant repudiation.

It is the oedipal disruption of mutual identification that establishes the complementary structure as the dominant residue of masculine infancy. It prevails through the organization of heterosexuality, which incarnates the formal fit between complementary subject-object relations and male-female relations — a virulent form of which is sustained in the aesthetization of

---

object's love to devaluation of the object. He mistranslates (1982) the famous phrase uttered by Herr K. in the Dora case: "I get nothing from my wife" (*habe*) as "My wife is nothing to me."

the passive feminine object. The sacrifices demanded by this form of complementarity include confinement to circumscribed gender identity as well as missed opportunities of intersubjectivity, the degradation of subject-to-subject relations between the sexes. These conditions appear not as a result but as an original cause: a woman or mother *is* this way, a man or father *is* that way. Hence, nothing seems more logical than the theorem that the mother's power over her dependent infant directly necessitates male dread and retaliation, even domination over women; no intervening explanation for this sequence seems necessary.

This theorem appears to work because it is predicated on the symbolic equation of mother with the repudiated but powerful object of identification and dreaded object of desire. And because the heterosexual complementarity continues to foreclose the intersubjective space in which communicative interaction might break up the equation, might differentiate it into symbol and symbolized. We have been able to deconstruct this equation, exposing its constitutive elements: envy and dread of maternal capacities and power, denigration of the mother-baby dyad, denial of feminine identifications and bisexual wishes, projection of aggression and retaliation into the other, reversal from passive to active, and the defensive displacement of omnipotence onto the idealized oedipal father — another symbolic equation.

Psychoanalytic theory uncritically reproduces the displacement of power in the notion of the father (or the third term that must not *be* the father but cannot simply be unlinked from its association with the father) as a force of differentiation.[7] In a kind

7. Some examples of this way of formulating the father's role can be found among such influential writers as Loewald (1980) and, of course, Chasseguet-Smirgel (1985). I realize that the Oedipus complex is not always interpreted in such a way as to stress the father-son relationship as one between subjects and the

of reversal, I have countered that this construction of the father may be a symbolic equation; that such concreteness actually reflects foreclosure of the potential space of symbolic intersubjectivity in the maternal dyad. My argument is not with the inclusion of the father as another other, a "second second," but with the unbending equation of the father with the third, a position that assumes both heterosexuality and a single normative form of family life. Furthermore, although maternal relatedness is defined in the oedipal model as a threat to masculinity, it is no more the essential prerogative of mother than of father (see Ruddick 1989). And although the appeal to the paternal symbolic equation may redefine the mutual intersubjectivity of mother and child as a regressive flight from reality, in fact that potential space can be recuperated by men as well as women. Despite the hegemony of the oedipal structure, the psyche preserves in various forms the legacy of early intersubjectivity, the alternate dyadic triangle of symbolization. Though partly occluded by idealization as well as by denigration, this symbolic field remains a powerful counterspace to that of oedipal complementarity.

But have we dispelled the clouds of idealization in this argument? Does this effort to reclaim intersubjectivity leave us in the mode of reversal, elevating the maternal at the expense of the paternal? Here we might recall Chodorow's (1979) argument, which contradicts the theorem that the mother's power necessitates male domination: that men have been able to in-

---

mother-son relationship as an objectifying one. Certainly, it has sometimes been crudely understood as love of mother and hatred of father. But such hatred, as analysis consistently reveals, is a particular way of identifying with father. Even when oedipal theory stresses not the boy's identification with the father but his rivalry or murderous impulses, we know that rivalry represents a kind of struggle to the death for recognition between subjects. Indeed, in Hegel's description of the struggle rivalry and identification are necessarily joined: rivalry is a way in which to identify with someone while remaining opposed to him.

stitute their chauvinism, their dread of the repudiated other, not because only males are in the position of envying and dreading the mother, not because only they are chauvinistic, but because they already have a position of power. As I have stated, the girl's oedipal position entails no less chauvinistic contempt, no less a repudiation of the masculine. Indeed, the oedipal girl's insistence on being the "little mother" — better known in kindergarten as the role of "little boss" — runs counter to the passive adoration of the male object and may be used to transform femininity into a triumphant assertion of superiority, a more successful way to capture power than the boy's identificatory love of the father. The unwillingness to relinquish the fantasy of maternal omnipotence, particularly when it is linked to the image of the sexually tantalizing, feminine object (as it tends to be in Latin or African-American culture), is readily apparent in women's defense of their traditionally exalted power to give and sustain life (see Dinnerstein 1976). And perhaps, as Dinnerstein argued, women's allegiance to maternal omnipotence plays a part in their acceptance of social submission — not in the sense of historical cause so much as its current inspiration. For without question, those who most idealize motherhood are those who most loudly defend the virtues of the paternal familial order. Is this not because the unconscious flip side of woman's embrace of maternal power is the mother's own feeling that she is a monster? Her terror of her power over her child, of the hatred mothers necessarily feel (Winnicott 1946; First 1994), inspires a wish to be controlled by a male counterpower.

Within feminism itself, we have seen an outpouring of women's writing that seeks to restore a lost maternal or feminine order on the margins of culture and to avoid the dark side of maternal power. This restoration avails itself of notions of preoedipal play, creativity and erotic life, the nonverbal representations of mutuality. It appeals, as I have done, to a different kind of symbolic space founded in intersubjectivity. The framing of this maternal order in opposition to the old paternal orders may justifiably be criticized as counteridealization (see Kristeva 1981). Yet we cannot simply extricate ourselves from these categorical oppositions; we can only establish a new relation to them. By way of conclusion, let me suggest that the feminist reversal has not remained a simple counteridealization but has begun to reformulate the opposition. If the feminist refiguring of the mother was a politically necessary moment, an effort to formulate what has been missing or lost, it did not remain there. It also led us deeper, uncovering the problematic relationship to the maternal ideal. I intend to show how such reversals of complementarity, as in the paradigmatic relation of mother and child, can be worked through to the point of reforming polarities into tensions.

First, we should note that the act of reversal that rejects the paternal ideal, like the defense of it, preserves a site of projected power that can be adhered to even in opposition. By opposing that power, one remains connected to it, borrows its charisma, and is ultimately seduced by it (see Gallop 1982). The phrase Butler (1995) used to characterize the melancholia of refused homosexual love — "I never loved him, I never lost him" — seems appropriate to the feminist repudiation of the father. It works not as a mourning that relinquishes the ideal but as a melancholia, a nostalgic denial and incorporation of what can neither be openly identified with nor relinquished. The melancholia in relation to the omnipotent paternal ideal, once the object of identificatory love, has often been uncritically refigured in the revaluations of the mother. Ironically, too, the creation of a reverse maternal ideal makes use of the whole cultural encoding of the paternal ideal, replete with ethical, epistemological, and psychological positions. It simply elevates all the denigrated poles of the binary opposition as women's virtues. In this form, the image of maternal redemption becomes another swing on the pendulum of power. Eventually such oscillations between complementary opposites create a hall-of-mirrors effect, in which maternal and paternal ideals become one another's "truth," then gradually through reciprocal reflection become indistinguishable.

Yet, in the evolution of feminist thought in recent years, the revaluation of the maternal ideal has not simply remained captive to the split complementarity. In a process resembling psychoanalysis, the transference to the preoedipal mother has "returned" many feminist thinkers, as mothers and daughters, to the deep conflicts that had been evaded by the idealization/defiance of the father. It faced them with the struggle for recognition, the problem of destruction and survival, the confrontation with imperfection, the conflict between idealizing the other and having one's own desire. No longer willing to escape this struggle for recognition through the heterosexual turn to the father, they discovered that the complementarity had to be reversed to the point where identification becomes reflexive. The current wave of feminist writing moved from the simple exaltation of maternal intersubjectivity to a fuller appreciation of the split-off aspect of the maternal ideal — in particular, the deep fear of destroying one's mother or child by separating.

This movement in current feminist thought has often been expressed in the self-reflections of the woman as writer, in which the conflict between mothering and finding one's own desire/subjectivity became acute. Because the woman writer — rather than, say, the political figure — has been so central, the conflict has been formulated in terms of the desire for the inner, not the outer, world. This effort to reclaim subjectivity became the occasion for the confrontation with the temptation of reverse idealization, the search for "the perfect mother" (Chodorow and Contratto 1982). The perfect mother of fantasy is the one who is always there, ready to sacrifice herself — and the child is not aware of the degree to which such a fantasy mother makes him or her feel controlled, guilty, envious, or unable to go away her- or himself. The child simply remains terrified of mother's leaving or of destroying her by becoming separate. In turn, the mother feels terrified of destroying her child by her own separation. Thus separation and guilt have often emerged as the axis of conflict for contemporary women writers. When the dangers of guilt-inspiring separation are seen as real rather than fantasized, space is foreclosed and the symbolic equation holds sway: the mother's child "is" the obstacle to her self-expression, and her self-expression "is" a threat to her child. The relationship is a zero-sum game.[8]

The writings of the feminist critic Susan Suleiman provide an evolving reflection on this problematic framework. At first, Suleiman illustrates the baldest expression of the terror of separation: "With every word I write, with every act of genuine creation, I hurt my child" (1985). Suleiman wants to show how this statement forecloses the space between reality and fantasy, so that the mother *is* to blame. Subsequently (1988), she investigates that foreclosure in an analysis of Mary Gordon's *Men and Angels*, a book that reaffirms the zero-sum stakes of a mother's choice and finds no way out of its harsh alternatives. A mother who chooses to pursue her own writing really does place her children at risk of death. Suleiman points out that this portrayal

8. Gallop (1989) gives a clever reading to a series of feminist texts on the mother-daughter relationship in which the mother's position is that of undifferentiation, giving her the appearance of "monster," while the daughter alone assumes the position of individuation. Overcoming the punitive psychoanalytic stance toward maternal narcissism requires an uncoupling of the position of individuation from the child. Gallop does not, however, imply that the position of individuation must actually be represented by a "third term," as her editors (Roof and Feldstein) suggest, but rather (in a riff that contrasts the symmetrical meeting of two "selfish" clitorides to the asymmetrical coupling of the phallus and container) that both members of the dyad may assume and co-create the individuating position.

depends upon unconsciously clinging to the image of a perfect mother and splitting the good mother from the bad "other mother." The other mother, the babysitter, takes on the indifference, selfishness, and hatred that are intolerable in the real mother, and she becomes the object of omnipotent rage who must be killed off. The book disavows the possibility that a "real" mother might acknowledge and deal with the strain (Kramer 1994) of her hatred for her children and their interference with her life.

Still later Suleiman (1990) tries to define a space that goes beyond the kill-or-be-killed world of omnipotence. She proposes that a mother might be represented who can play with her child and thus be recognized "most fully as a subject — autonomous and free . . . able to take the risk of 'infinite expansion' that goes with creativity," a mother who can open up the symbolic space of play. She offers a vision of "boys (later to be men)" who actually enjoy seeing their mother move instead of sitting motionless, "a peaceful center around which the child weaves his play [Barthes]; of girls (later to be women) who learn that they do not have to grow up to be motionless mothers" (p. 180).

The difficult task this sets feminist consciousness is to imagine how a woman, as daughter or mother, can transform the space of inevitable separation and loss into a space of creation and play. Jane Lazarre, whose account of a stormy young motherhood, *The Mother Knot*, conveyed the entrapment in the symbolic equation of separation with destruction or death, has more recently sought to deconstruct that equation, in which the mother must sacrifice her children or her self. Her later book, *Worlds Beyond My Control*, takes its title from Sara Ruddick's important book, *Maternal Thinking* (1989): "To give birth is to create a life that cannot be kept safe, whose unfolding cannot be controlled, and whose eventual death is certain. . . . In a world beyond one's control to be humble is to have a profound sense of the limits of one's actions and of the unpredictability of the consequences of one's work."

Lazarre portrays the mother's struggle to accept this condition by exploring the daughter's fantasy of perfection, her blame of her own mother, and her determination to outdo her by being the truly good mother. Lazarre's character no longer defines her children as an obstacle to her writing, or her writing as an obstacle to her mothering. She realizes, instead, that her obstacle is the dream of perfect symmetry, her own wish to be completely recognized, completely responded to — her fantasy of perfect self-expression in a perfect world. Her challenge is to continue writing, loving, seeking recognition, in the absence of the fantasy mother-redeemer who would constitute that world. She comes to realize that she cannot re-create that mother either in her writing or in her efforts to protect her own children from the world. Rather, she has to find a way to contain, through writing, the loss of an illusion that was common to both the "pristine beginning" of her writing and her "newborn's unscarred flesh": the illusion that she would achieve "the perfect reparation." It is not only the dissolution/disillusion of this fantasy but the author's ownership of those ideal images as her own creation (see Eigen 1993) that has brought the struggle with the maternal figure closer to the point beyond reparation. For something lies beyond the mother and her loss — something we learn to reach as we bridge loss through symbolic experience — and, as Eigen (1981) writes, that is "the unknowable ground of creativeness" that the transitional space provides.

For this reason, it is not enough to renounce such fantasies, equating their deconstruction with the bitter disillusionment that turns us against ourselves, chastising ourselves as victims of false hope, of a childish longing for redemption. Nor does disillusionment alone constitute a real base for the knowledge of difference. By itself, it reflects only the disparagement of what was once loved, the countering of mania with depression, the refusal to mourn concealed by the repudiation of all longing. The alternative to a defensive fantasy of omnipotence is the labor of mourning, which requires the solidarity of the witnessing other (see Santner 1990). And mourning, in turn, invites the other. It gives rise to gestures of reparation that, accepting the imperfection, the inaccuracy, all the misses in our reach for the other, can lead to restoration of the expressive space of resonance with that other. As I have said, it would be good enough for that space to be freed of coercive reconciliations by surviving the tests of destruction and difference — for us to sometimes endure and sometimes enjoy the other's outside existence. And if we cannot expect to eradicate the deep, unconscious sediment of the omnipotence fantasy in our psychic and cultural life, it might be good enough to know how we might mitigate its most dire forms: by taking that fantasy back into the self, owning our capacity to create a realm of the ideal. Within the space between survival and loss, acknowledging our own propensity for adoration and dread, fantasy can become the medium of the self at play. That space of creative interchange offers consolation for the inevitable experience of leaving and losing the other, of not being, or having, everything.

4 / Father and Daughter, Identification with Difference: A Contribution to Gender Heterodoxy

Since the 1970s most of Freud's views on feminine development have been subjected to critical revision. Where Freud (1933) saw the girl beginning life as "a little man," most analysts now regard the girl's early attachment to her mother as a bond of identification that fosters her femininity. Numerous papers have disputed Freud's (1925, 1931, 1933) main contentions: that girls are not aware of their own genitals, that they do not develop a firm superego, that they are more guided by envy of the opposite sex than boys. More generally, a new theory of gender identity has been evolving (Stoller 1968; Chodorow 1978; Person and Ovesey 1983; Fast 1984), one that views gender development as a relational process involving identification and separation issues. This new paradigm of gender not only corrects the flagrant depreciation of women but offers an explanation of developmental difficulties that boys as well as girls must negotiate. It offers a notion of gender that is not motivated by, although it does encompass, genital difference.

This essay originally appeared in *Psychoanalytic Dialogues* 1 (1991):277–299. Used by permission.

However, the new paradigm is in some respect at odds with current feminist theorizing, which has been produced largely outside the auspices of psychoanalysis in academic disciplines, notably literature and philosophy. That feminist theoretical approach questions the notion of unitary gender identity and challenges our acceptance of gender as a binary system (see Dimen 1991; Goldner 1991). Once this system is questioned, femininity and masculinity are no longer seamless categories; indeed, they are barely adequate to contain their volatile, sometimes explosive, subject matter. The confrontation between gender identity theory and this radical critique of gender categories may help to push our thinking into further unexplored territory.

I am going to suggest that the paradigm of gender identity can then expand to include flexible and metaphoric reinterpretations of the emblems of sexual difference. For example, once we question the goal of a normative "femininity" that excludes all elements of "masculinity," once we are aware of the opposing gendered aspects every self must negotiate, penis envy may become interesting again in a new way. The contemporary psychoanalytic mainstream seems to have accepted the clinical reinterpretation of penis envy as a "developmental metaphor" (Grossman and Stewart 1977), but the possibilities of this metaphor have only begun to be explored. Actually, penis envy could become a kind of metaphor for the development of theory: its expanded capacity to represent multiple meanings and to allow multiple interpretations over time exemplifies the decentering of our method. Its wider epistemological implication would be to challenge notions of correct interpretation and definitive meaning, notions that have given way before the postmodern tide of uncertainty in all the related disciplines, especially regarding gender. In this essay, I will offer a new developmental analysis of penis envy, and I will try to show how this perspective on development opens the way to accepting the multiplicity of meanings and interpretations of gender that appear in clinical work.

As you recall, for Freud, envy of the penis required no further explanation — it *was* the explanation. It provided a simple, elegant answer to a central question: how does the girl turn to her father and enter her Oedipus complex? The girl in the genital phase, primed by her focus on the clitoris as an active organ, instantaneously recognizes the superiority of the penis and, resentful of her mother, turns to the father, from whom she may finally hope to gain the penis or its substitute, the baby. With this turn to a passive relation to the father and his phallus, the music stops and the girl is without a chair.

But those who dissented from Freud's original opinion — especially Horney (1924, 1933a), Jones (1927, 1933), and Klein (1928) — saw penis envy as a phenomenon to be explained. They never disputed the existence of this phenomenon, observable in little girls, but they disagreed that the superiority of the penis was so self-evident as to require no further thought. Why should a girl's envy of the penis exceed the narcissistic wish to possess everything, parallel to a boy's wish for breasts or babies? Both Klein and Horney argued that girls had much to cherish in their anticipation of motherhood and fertility. At the same time, Freud's question — Why does the little girl give up her mother and turn to love the father? — did appear to have a self-evident answer. Assuming heterosexuality, they attributed to the little girl knowledge about her vagina and its complementarity to the penis; consequently, the girl desires to have that place in relation to father that mother now has.

Perhaps, Horney (1924, 1926) theorized, penis envy becomes salient only when the little girl backs off from father love, fears competing with mother, and chooses instead to identify with father. Thus penis envy would not be the trigger of the

Oedipus complex, as Freud thought, but indeed the result of a misfired oedipal situation, a "flight from womanhood." The perception of her own organs as damaged or inadequate might occur, Horney and Klein agreed, because the little girl fears injury as retribution for her envious wish to supplant mother by stealing her father's penis or injure her by stealing her babies. Klein's sense of the multiple meanings of penis envy remains clinically interesting and fresh, and Horney's work in particular deserves to be rescued from the disparagement it received from the psychoanalytic establishment. But it should be noted that Horney and Klein answered Freud's original question about the switch to the father in a rather Freudian way, by their own appeals to anatomical destiny (see J. Mitchell 1974).

It was not until psychoanalysis produced a more developed theory of identification and relocated the development of sexual difference in a much earlier period that the questions of both Freud and his critics could be reframed. At that point it became possible to explicate the importance of identifications, unconscious as well as conscious, in the formation of gender (Stoller 1968; Chodorow 1978; Fast 1984).

The idea of gender identity development did not, however, raise gender or genitality into a conscious, conflict-free zone, as some defenders of Freud's position feared. Rather, it moved the struggle with gender difference back into the preoedipal period of separation-individuation; this shift offered the possibility of reinterpreting genital and other bodily preoccupations in light of conflicts in self-development and object relations. This theoretical vantage point can now reframe some of the dissenters' ideas as well. Take, for example, the flight from womanhood, which Horney used to explain the persistence of penis envy (or the masculinity complex), the girl's insistence on being like the father rather than having him heterosexually. While Horney thought that the girl was retreating from an oedipal threat, we might also see this as a preoedipal move to resolve difficulties in separation by repudiating identification with the mother and identifying with father.

Current reinterpretations of penis envy have emphasized the girl's need to identify with the father as a figure of separation from the preoedipal mother. Emphasizing the power of the preoedipal mother and early object relations, the French analysts MacDougall (1980) and Chasseguet-Smirgel (1970) and the American feminists Chodorow (1978) and Dinnerstein (1976) concur that the power of the father and his phallus derives from their meaning in separating from mother. The French analysts see this "beating back the mother" (Chasseguet-Smirgel) as a response to early maternal omnipotence and helplessness, in particular the anally controlling mother. Representing difference and separation, the phallus becomes the desired object for children of both sexes. The meaning of the penis as a symbol of revolt and separation derives from the nature of the child's struggle to separate from the original maternal power.

The father, not the phallus, then becomes the point of departure for our interpretation — the father as he is represented internally, refracted through the conflicts that are currently dominant in the child's psyche. I have suggested that in the period of maximal separation conflict — in rapprochement — a representation of the father emerges that is significant for both boys and girls (Benjamin 1986, 1988). The psychological imperatives of early narcissism and separation-individuation lead the child to invest the father and the phallus with idealized attributes. These idealized attributes are crucial not only to self but also to sexual development.

Although psychoanalytic theory has given far less weight to the father than to the mother in the preoedipal period, it has generally recognized the importance of the father as a figure of identification for the boy. Father is crucial because the boy has been parented primarily by a woman; the boy needs, in Greenson's (1968) terms, to disidentify with mother in order to separate and assume his masculinity (Stoller 1973). In conjunction with this view, some writers on male development (Blos 1984; Tyson 1986) have stressed the importance for the boy of the loved, not rivalrous, preoedipal or dyadic father. In *Group Psychology and the Analysis of the Ego*, Freud noted the importance of the dyadic father in "the early history" of the Oedipus complex: "A boy will exhibit a special interest in his father; he would like to grow like him and be like him, and take his place everywhere. . . . He takes his father as his ideal." This father of identification is beginning to be recognized as crucial to early separation and self-development; a boy's difficulties in separation are often traced to the father's unavailability for identification in this phase. However, no comparable value is given to the father as an object in the girl's life and inner world, especially at this period. Only a few women analysts have given thought to the implications of this fact for girls (Bernstein 1983; Lax 1977; Clower 1977; Levenson 1984; Spieler 1984).

Abelin (1980), developing Mahler's position, has shown how the father's differences from the mother first assume salience for the child in the rapprochement phase, when gender difference and genital difference begin to be recognized. At that point the struggle to differentiate becomes fatefully intertwined with the consolidation of gender identity (see Mahler, Pine, and Bergmann 1975). This period involves not only separation anxiety, loss, or loss of omnipotence but also the struggle for recognition, particularly the difficult matter of being recognized as independent by the one you were dependent upon. The child is becoming conscious of intention, will, and agency in a new way: mother leaving, for example, is not only about tolerating separation but about recognizing that mother will not do as one wishes. At this point the child not only needs but also wants—

by this I mean that he or she self-consciously wills to have or do something. The child needs to eat, for example, but wants — even demands — to eat from the bowl with the clown picture. In each concrete expression of want lies a general wish to be recognized as a subject of desire rather than merely subject to a need. Rapprochement inaugurates the first of many such struggles to effect one's intent and be recognized in one's desire, many of which will carry the imprint of this first paradigmatic struggle.

At this point, also, gender and genital difference begin to be registered, and the difference between mother and father begins to take hold symbolically in the psyche. As the conflict between the fear of separation and the desire to be independent comes to a head, the contradiction between security and autonomous will often feels unmanageable. The two irreconcilable needs then begin to be formulated as a gender split: mother represents attachment and father the recognition of independence. This assumes, of course, traditional gender divisions in parenting, where mother is the primary nurturing figure, associated with dependency, inside, security. However, even in the increasing number of families that do not reproduce this stereotype, we can often observe the creation of a fantasy father-hero who represents the link to the exciting outside and assumes the role of standing for freedom, separation, and desire. This does not mean, however, that psychic changes will not follow from changes in parenting and gender organization. Psychic structure evolves through the interaction of internal and external worlds. When the mother is the "coming and going," outside parent, the structure may be reversed (Pruett 1987); a little boy, for example, may manifest a much greater insistence on likeness with his mother, even on having the same anatomy or appearance that she does. However, this reversed gender structure would probably not mesh with the culturally dominant representations of "outside" encountered a bit later — male media heroes, for example — and thus would not yield such an *apparent* coherence of gender identity as the traditional model does. For that matter, I do not believe that gender identity is really coherent at this point or that most boys need to or do disidentify with mother. The assumption that they do derives from the questionable proposition that early identification with mother is gendered (Stoller 1973; see also Person and Ovesey 1983). I suspect that boys at this point do become more separate and simultaneously begin to differentiate paternal from maternal, adding and organizing aspects of the father in a more integrated and distinct way.

As Abelin explains it, the child, who now needs to be able to represent himself as a subject who desires, does so by forming a symbolic representation of another subject with whom he or she can identify. The father offers the boy toddler his first model of desire, and the boy now imagines himself to *be* the father, the subject of desire, in relation to the mother. While Abelin attributes central importance to the wish, "I want Mommy," I believe that this declaration is a telescoping of oedipal and pre-oedipal reactions, based largely on a case in which a new sibling took the mother away. Mahler's interpretation (1966, cited in Abelin 1980) is more fundamental, that the father is a "knight in shining armor" because he comes from "outer space" and brings the excitement of outsideness, uncontaminated by conflicts around dependency.

In any event, the father now represents a different kind of object — a subject — who is not so much the source of goodness as the mirror of desire. He represents a subject who can want and act appropriately to fill those wants. The child gains from him not merely *direct recognition* through approval or confirmation, but recognition through *symbolic identification* with this powerful subject who is his or her ideal. In a sense, the father's entry is a deus ex machina that solves the rapprochement dilemma of having to get the confirmation of one's independence from the person one still longs to depend upon. Identification with the father is a vehicle for avoiding conflict as well as for separation, for denying helplessness and the loss of practicing grandiosity. In the boy's mind, the magical father with whom he identifies is still omnipotent, as he would like to be (and as mother might be). Recognition through identification, and its elaboration in fantasy, is now substituted for the more conflictual need to be recognized by the primary parent with whom he feels his dependency. Of course the child identifies with, looks for recognition from, and attributes omnipotence to both parents at this time. But whereas the mother's power appears to lie in control over the child and may be "contaminated" by the child's enmeshment with her, the power of the exciting father lies more in his relation to the world outside, beyond maternal power.

The affirmed identification with father, then, has a double aspect: on the one hand, a denial of rapprochement helplessness, on the other hand, a confirmation of the core experience of being the subject of desire. On the one hand, the identificatory impulse functions defensively to avoid the ambivalent mother; on the other, the wish to be like father expresses an intrinsic need to make desire one's own, to experience it as legitimate and self-originated, not as the property of the object, but as one's own inner desire. Thus many facets of the child's development may now impel her or him toward the father as a symbolic figure of recognition — the need to separate, the need to avoid ambivalence, and the need to find a subject who represents desire and excitement.

Speaking more generally, one upshot of this interpretation of the father is to acknowledge that identification plays a key role in love and desire. Identification, being like, is the chief mode in which a child of this age can acknowledge the subjectivity of another person. Identification is not merely an internal process, it is also a kind of relationship: Freud (1921) actually described identification as the first emotional tie to the object before he finalized its place as the precipitate of abandoned object cathexes (1923). Peculiar to this phase of development, then, is a kind of *identificatory love*. This relationship of identification is with someone outside and different from the first object, someone who is a subject, not a source of goodness. Identificatory love is the relational context in which, for males, separation and gender identification occur. The strong mutual attraction between father and son allows for recognition through identification, a special erotic relationship. The practicing toddler's "love affair with the world" turns into a homoerotic love affair with the father, who represents the world. The boy is in love with his ideal. This homoerotic, identificatory love serves as the boy's vehicle of establishing masculine identity and confirms his sense of himself as subject of desire.

Of course, this process of identification can be successful only when it is reciprocal, when the father identifies with his son and makes himself available to him. And fathers, it seems, do respond to their sons' need for identification more positively than to their daughters'. Fathers have preferred their boy infants, forming a more intense bond based on identification, which is followed by greater mutual attachment and mutual identification in toddlerhood (Lamb 1977; Gunsberg 1982). For its part, psychoanalytic theory has uncritically reflected this reality. It has made the girl's relationship to the father, in contrast to the boy's, hinge on the phallus rather than on identification. The girl's desire surfaces in a defensive, part-object context. In fact, identification with the father has no structured place in the girl's preoedipal development comparable to that of the boy's relationship to the mother. The observation that little girls in rapprochement become more depressed and lose more of their practicing enthusiasm than boys is linked by Mahler, Pine, and Bergmann (1975) to recognition of the anatomical difference. And of course, Roiphe and Galenson (1981) wrote a book on the early genital phase in order to advance that proposition. Abelin (1980), too, argues that the father plays a small part for the girl — perhaps, he says, because of her penis envy. In this view, the father's unavailability is secondary, contingent upon the girl's castration reaction — that is, her recognition of anatomical difference.

My argument is just the opposite. The rapprochement girl's wish for a penis is not a self-evident response to anatomical difference. She desires it even as the boy cherishes it (or will come to cherish it): because she is struggling to individuate. Girls seek what toddler boys recognize in their fathers and wish, through identification, to affirm in themselves — recognition of their own desire. And their ambivalence around separation may be more intense than that of boys because of the bond of likeness between mother and daughter. All the more reason for them, too, to seek a different object in whom to recognize their independence. This other object is very often the father, whose otherness is guaranteed and symbolized by his other genital. Precisely when this father is unavailable, envy of the penis expresses the girl's longing for him.

Even Galenson and Roiphe (1982), in their effort to prove that the girl's rapprochement depression derives from a castration reaction, inadvertently provide only examples of girls who miss their absent fathers. They sum up one little girl's longing for a departed father by saying, "the missing excitement and erotic nature of their relationship, which had earlier been attached to the father in toto, was now identified as emanating from his phallus in particular" (p. 162). Mahler, Pine, and Bergmann (1975) report a similar case of a girl, Cathy, whose father is away and who begins to express envy of a little boy's penis during that time. No doubt, the transformation from excitement and desire in general to the (unattainable) phallus does begin here, especially enhanced when the father himself is missing. But this clamoring for the symbol expresses the loss behind the rapprochement depression — it does not cause it.

Still, we might ask, can the girl, through a more positive identification with the father, resolve this difficulty and come to feel that desire and agency are properly hers? Ideally, we look forward to the evolution of a cultural context and familial constellations that allow girls (and boys) to identify with a mother who is outside as well as inside, who can represent subjectivity just as well as the father. But in the familial culture which is characterized by a traditional gender division, daughters have tried (and will probably continue to try) to use paternal identification in this way. However misinterpreted, the fact of penis envy does testify to this effort. But for psychoanalytic theory the question remains, could a more positive father-daughter relationship in fact allow a different integration of identification? This question points to the broader theoretical issue: the need to decenter the notion of gender identification, so that it refers to the plurality of developmental positions rather than to a unilinear line of development, which is ultimately referable to the anatomical difference. I propose that children use cross-sex identifications to formulate important parts of their self representations as well as to elaborate fantasies about sexual relations (to fill out the character of the other in their sexual dramas, for example). Supporting this proposition is Fast's theory of gender differentiation, which suggests that children initially do not recognize that certain possibilities are excluded because of anatomical difference. Children in the preoedipal phase are "overinclusive"; they believe they can have or be everything. For both sexes, identifications with both parents continue until the oedipal recognition of sexual complementarity precipitates a crisis of loss and renunciation. The sense of self and secondary characteristics that are integrated through these identifications may continue even when specific, opposite-sex capacities are renounced.

In fact, a careful study of gender differentiation suggests that there are more phases and more tension between inclusion and exclusion than psychoanalytic theory has yet recognized. Once core gender identity is established in the first twelve to eighteen months of life, the child proceeds to elaborate gender role identity in conjunction with separation-individuation issues, hence in a conflictual and variable context (Person and Ovesey 1983). Children continue throughout the second and third years to identify with both parents, even though their roles are somewhat differentiated and the father may assume special importance. Toward the end of the overinclusive pre-oedipal phase, the child shows simultaneous awareness of the limits of gender (complementarity) and a determined protest against them (Fast 1984): this is the period of penis envy and pregnancy envy par excellence. Here castration fear means being robbed of what the other sex has. As the oedipal phase begins, as the child realizes he or she can be only one thing, an overly rigid notion of complementarity and a repudiation of the opposite sex sets in. This early oedipal stance is marked by the defense against loss and envy: sour grapes, but also romance — the heteroerotic desire for the idealized Other. It is at this time that castration anxiety begins to mean, for girls as well as boys, loss of one's own genitals (Mayer 1985). Later on in the oedipal phase (or in the adolescent replay), both castration fear and repudiation of the opposite sex can be toned down. Ideally this allows for reintegration of cross-sex identifications and access to a transitional use of overinclusiveness (Bassin 1994) — a happy outcome which, for reasons I have discussed elsewhere (Benjamin 1988), most notably the disparagement and subjugation of women, can by no means be taken for granted.

In any event, it is important to differentiate those longings and anxieties related to the rapprochement father identification from heterosexual feelings that appear in the oedipal phase. The assumption has too often been made that the girl's preoedipal interest in her father, because erotic, is heterosexual. But the interest in the penis at this phase is not heterosexual, it is not about uniting or reuniting with father or mother; it is about homoerotic incorporation, about having something that competes with the powerful breast. It is a homoerotic desire, a desire for likeness, that often resurfaces in the latency wish to be a buddy. The complex nature of the father-daughter relationship has often been obscured by analytic acceptance of the fallacy that all opposite-sex love is heterosexual. As Harris (1991) pointed out in her discussion of Freud's "Case of Homosexuality in a Woman," whether a loved object is perceived as different or like, whether it is a hetero- or a homoerotic choice, is not determined merely by the object's sex. To assume that it is so determined would be, to borrow a phrase, to do psychoanalysis in the missionary position.

Each love object embodies multiple possibilities of sameness and difference, of masculinity and femininity, and one love relationship may serve a multitude of functions. In each relationship the axis of similarity and complementarity is aligned somewhat differently with the axis of gender. Paradoxically, one may love the Other who appears to be different in order to be or become more like him or her: through incorporation and assimilation in our fantasy, as well as through loving recognition by the person we take as our ideal, we hope eventually to become that ideal. "The female tendency to love the embodiment of her own sacrificed ego ideal in the man" (Jacobsen 1937) was recognized by early women analysts like Jacobsen and Reich (1940) but explained psychosexually as founded in a wish to orally incorporate the penis. My argument is the reverse — that the incorporation is a means of becoming the ideal object rather than an end in itself.

The father, then, can be an object of homoerotic love for the girl. This homoerotic love, impelled by the developmental force of separation, may indeed lead the way into a later heterosexuality. At the beginning of the oedipal phase, when she confronts the exclusivity of genital difference and realizes that she cannot be or have everything, the girl may switch from homo- to heteroerotic love; she may choose to love in men the masculinity that she once wished to have in herself. Still, this love will be less tainted with submission and guilt to the degree that her identificatory love has been recognized: she will not have to steal or envy his masculinity. It is also true that a girl's oedipal conflicts and striving to be the stereotyped heterosexual object may mask or negate her earlier striving for identificatory love, especially if it was unsuccessful. But the rapprochement phase, even with its incipient recognition of the genital difference, is not yet the Oedipus complex.

Here I would like to address some of the main consequences of disappointment in identificatory love of the father. I have argued (Benjamin 1986, 1988) that the idealization of the phallus and the wish for a missed identificatory love with father inspire adult women's fantasies about loving men who represent their ideal. The early deflation of omnipotence in daughters who miss their father's recognition may, as some analysts appear to think, have its rewards in ego development and identification with mother; but too often such daughters wind up admiring the men who get away with their grandiosity intact. As mothers, they may become especially indulgent and proud of their sons' grandiosity. Or they may express this admiration (concealing unconscious envy or resentment) in a special kind of relationship to their ideal, often tinged with service or submission, sometimes sexual masochism. The adult woman's ideal love scenarios often show identificatory, homoerotic themes, where a woman is finally recognized by the one who represents the subject she would like to be. There is a genre of male-female adventure films that expresses this fantasy, in which sexual romance can be achieved only after the success of a cooperative venture in which the woman displays or assimilates much of the man's abilities and daring.

A confirmed recognition from the father — "yes, you can be like me" — helps the child consolidate the identification and so enhances the sense of being a subject of desire. But the lack of recognition and the denial of the identificatory bond damage the sense of being a sexual subject and lead the woman to look for her desire through a man — and frequently lead to masochistic fantasies of surrendering to the ideal man's power. The search for identificatory love is thematic in many relationships of submission. (This is true not only of women with men, but also, of course, of male submission to more powerful, older males; the search for a father of identification culminating in a deferential or submissive relationship is very typical for men in adolescence or young adulthood.) As fathers, these same men may remain distant from their sons in order to defend against what they feel to be the sadistic character of the homoerotic bond — reflecting their own anger and masochism toward their fathers.[1]

---

1. Male submission rooted in frustrating relations with a withdrawn or unavailable father has similar dynamics. I have been asked whether it isn't the father's withdrawal of tender object love from the child that encourages the transformation of the boy's object love into identification. In my view, however, the urge to identify is not simply a precipitate of relinquished object love but rather a constant tendency alongside object love. One might say that if the object love is withdrawn, the child's identification changes its character, becoming submissive and idealizing, even masochistic. A father whose own father was distant might prematurely perceive closeness through the screen of oedipal relations — aggressive rivalry and

In line with this perspective on women's submission, I have also suggested that the daughter's homoerotic love of the father might shed light on Freud's (1919) discussion of the masturbation fantasy, "A Child Is Being Beaten." One aspect that puzzled Freud at first was that the girl's fantasy always depicted a boy being beaten by the father and that it was the boy with whom she masochistically identified. Freud concluded that girls used a boy in the fantasy because they were turning away from the incestuous love of the father, which "spurs their masculinity complex" (a phrase he used here for the first time). I propose, rather, that the beaten child had to be a boy because the fantasy of being the father's son was in fact the central frustrated wish. The humiliation associated with the disappointment of this wish was expressed in the sexually exciting punishment — a humiliation that was likely to be iatrogenically intensified by the misunderstanding of penis envy and the condemnation of the masculinity complex in the "dark ages" of psychoanalysis.

A striking illustration of how the wish to be the father's son might underlie the woman's masochistic fantasy can be found in an analysis of the origins of Freud's essay. Young-Bruehl, in her biography of Anna Freud (1988), contends that Anna was actually the patient upon whom Freud based much of this material. Because Anna was in analysis with her father during this period and wrote a paper on beating fantasies three years later in order to be admitted to the Vienna Psychoanalytic Society, at a time when she was not yet seeing patients, Young-Bruehl concludes that both her paper and Freud's thesis were based upon her own

(negative oedipal) homosexual submission — and therefore withdraw in this way. This withdrawal, however, exacerbates the son's transformation of the erotic into aggressive impulses, as well as his idealization of the more distant father, thus re-creating a paternal identification tinged with submission and the tendency toward sadomasochism in relations with men — a process not unlike the transformation of identificatory love into masochism that I describe in women.

analysis. And Anna Freud also fit the profile of the patient described in her paper, who, to replace the earlier beating fantasies, obsessively created what she called "nice stories" in which younger men were punished by older men; she, too, finally successfully sublimated these into stories of male heroes. The story of Anna's rebelliousness against her mother's control, her struggle against masturbation and the obsessional "stories," her place at her father's side, her use of this paper to gain admission to her father's world, and indeed Freud's own confession that he would "feel like Junius Brutus the elder when he had to judge his own son" (cited in Young-Bruehl, p. 108)—all suggest how the wish to be son to her father, a forbidden homoerotic love, might underlie that sexual fantasy. In any event, the happy ending was that Anna's paper was accepted, and when one of the members said that Anna's patient was "totally abnormal," her father came to her rescue and "defended her little girl" (p. 108). Is it possible that this solution, Freud's acceptance of Anna as his "son," helped her to resolve her struggle with the masochistic, sexual form of this fantasy?

It is also worth noting that Freud's 1919 paper essentially proposed the same argument, which Horney later elaborated in "The Flight from Womanhood" (1926): that the girl regresses from her genital incestuous love into a masculine identification. This premise raises again the question of which motive comes first, identification or object love, and how to disentangle the two. This has always been a tricky question, even for Freud: on the one hand, identification was the earliest emotional tie to the object; on the other, it was the precipitate of object relations. But the problem could be solved by decentering our explanation and saying, "All of the above." It seems generally likely that, by the time she has reached adulthood, the daughter's identification as her father's son would incorporate multiple motives, no two of them mutually exclusive—that identification could express a defense against heterosexual involvement with father, or a defensive repudiation of the mother, or, again, an unsatisfied wish for identificatory love complicated by rejection, humiliation, and punishment. The formal problem in our theory has been the insistence on *one* motive, usually oedipal; the substantive problem has been conflating the fantasy of pain with the desire for pain and thus missing the real wish — for a close, identificatory bond with the father — and the humiliation associated with rejection.

Psychoanalysts have generally assumed that the positive father transference of their women patients is oedipal, heterosexual in content. The longing to identify with the idealized father of separation — to be empowered, to be separate from mother, and to feel excited — appeared in the guise of penis envy and was interpreted as resistance to oedipal feelings, or it was simply conflated with oedipal wishes ("you want to have my baby"). Psychoanalysts also interpreted the idealized father transference of male patients, or the urge to submit to father in order to incorporate the phallus, as a negative oedipal stance (an identification with a passive mother) rather than as an expression of the longing to recognize themselves in and be recognized by the early dyadic father.

This reinterpretation of oedipal material and penis envy fits well with some of the case material in recent literature. For example, Kohut (1977) recounts the reanalysis of a case in which penis envy played a significant role (although Kohut's alignment of mirroring with the mother and cohesion with the father does not capture the role of the father as mirror of desire). The patient, Miss V., dreamed that she was standing urinating over a toilet and that someone was watching her from behind. (Interestingly, Horney [1924] cites a woman who had a similar formulation, "I am urinating like my father, standing up," as her chief masturbation fantasy.) Kohut tells us that Miss

V.'s previous analyst had made repeated attempts to get her to recognize that her hopelessness stemmed from her futile wish to get the penis. He concluded instead that this dream and her wish to see the father's penis stemmed from a need to "extricate herself from her relation with her bizarre and emotionally shallow mother and turn toward her emotionally more responsive and down-to-earth father" (p. 221). I would add that this turn to the father may not only be a defense against mother, necessitated by mother's inadequacy, but also reflects a developmentally appropriate wish to be seen by the father (the analyst) as like him. Furthermore, the defensive direction (away from mother) should not eclipse the erotic direction (toward father), which reflects the original eroticism of identificatory love.

I would speculate that the more confirmation and the less humiliation a girl meets when she tries to fulfill the wish for identificatory love, the more the wish emerges free of self-abnegating or masochistic elements. For example, the wish was articulated in the dream of a married woman who was involved in an intense ideal love of an admired mentor. He treated her as a favorite student, indeed as a daughter, inviting her to spend time with him and his wife and encouraged her work, which progressed accordingly. She dreamed that she was masturbating while speaking to someone who, she reflected on waking, must certainly have been the mentor. The words she uttered were, "I want to be your little boy."

In a case reported by Bernstein (1983), the wish to be the father's son emerged in the transference to a woman analyst. The patient dreamed that she appeared at the analyst's office dressed as a boy, "feeling sort of sheepish but [I] seem to be asking you if it is okay." The patient's associations were of "fathers who wanted their sons to follow in their footsteps, sons who wanted to be like their fathers," and her family's differential treatment of herself and her brother. Bernstein concludes that "her need was acute for her father . . . to recognize and encourage her professional aspirations, to permit identification" (p. 196). She warns that this move toward the analyst is often misinterpreted as erotic rather than recognized as a wish for identification. Indeed, this may be because the wish for identification often appears as erotic. If the transference is often misinterpreted, it is not only because the identificatory impulse is missed but because eros is so narrowly understood — as if "erotic" meant only oedipal-genital aspirations, or love of what is different; as if eros did not infuse the desire to be like. What may be confusing, of course, is that common to both sorts of erotic transference manifestations are shame and the star-struck yearning for what is near but yet so far.

The displacement of the beating fantasy in tales of an adventurous male hero, as in Anna Freud's stories, or the later fusion of the two in sexual submission to such heroes (as in dime-store gothic novels) is another common variant of identificatory love. Then again, the fantasy of being the assistant or sidekick may fuse with more heteroerotic elements in a less humiliating romance. For example, a woman reported seeing again the movie version of "Robin Hood," which had been the basis for her most exciting childhood daydreams, and finding it "perfect." She was delighted by many of the movie's themes, not least that in the moment of acknowledging her love, Maid Marian declares to Robin Hood her intention to become his accomplice, to spy on the bad king, to help the good king back to his throne. Robin Hood himself is thrilling because he is an outlaw (a rebellious boy, perhaps a brother, thus a figure of separation from maternal power), a fabulous archer, who is yet a helper to the poor (the children) and on the side of the good. The relationship is ultimately sanctioned by the king, who orders Robin to marry Maid Marian; she gets the paternal approval but marries the ideal brother/son, who is not yet an oedipal authority, not the patriarchal father, who might dominate or disparage mother.

I will conclude my argument for a more complex understanding of gender identification and its role in erotic life with an illustration of how identificatory love may appear in the transference and in related fantasy or dream material. Identificatory love may become manifest in different ways, switching between men and women, father and brother, sexual and nonsexual. In this case a woman had a very strong, in many ways loving, tie to her mother; however, this tie was ambivalently experienced as restrictive and controlling: she had always felt she must not be unfaithful to mother. All of her sexual fantasies and crushes devolved on younger men, boys, who, she readily admitted, were exactly who she would be or would want to be if she were a male. For some time she had a crush on a gay colleague and in one session reported a dream that she was making love with him. She concluded the session by talking about having a secret. At the beginning of the next session she returned to the theme of the secret. The association was that in preadolescence she used to explore sexual matters with a girlfriend, doing such things as looking at *Playboy*. One time when they were talking about the penises of the stars of "Star Trek," the friend said, "Speaking of that, your fly is open."

The third session opened with an account of a dream about the boots that her older brother gave her for Christmas. She told me that they were exactly like a pair of boots that I had — a fact that she remembered only upon recounting the dream. She considered the boots very stylish, and they fit well — typical of her brother's ability to get wonderful presents one doesn't dare get for oneself. In the dream, she returned the boots for some unspecified reason, getting a larger size, but the replacements did not look as good: they were too high, came up over the knee, so that they looked like someone else's boots. She then explained that her brother had also given her mother a purse for Christmas, but mother had found it too kittenish, too small, and had returned it for a larger, more practical one. She then speculated that in the dream it might have been her mother who had made her exchange the boots, even though the original pair fit.

This woman's primary relation with mother forbade separation and having her own desire. The boots were a gift from the brother, who had a miraculous ability to recognize her desire; they were, moreover, a means of identifying with the analyst. (Did I represent the one who had her own desire, who was unattainable and idealized like the brother, or was I the mother, with the too-big boots?) The boots were both a feminine container and a phallus, thus representing male and female desire: "stylish" — i.e., feminine — as well as "very apropos," which echoed the "speaking of that" and the penises of the stars. The bigger boots, like the bigger purse, were not sexy but practical: the sign of the phallic mother, representing not desire but control or engulfment. As the patient put it, her mother would let her have a penis, but not a sexy one. A penis that represents desire is something that men have; she believes that sexuality is something the man confers with his penis.

The duality of these images, the masculine and feminine nature of the boots, is essential. It suggests the layering of meanings and wishes from different phases, which are often condensed in one fantasy, image, or screen memory, and reveal themselves at different points in the analysis. The dream shows how the phallus can represent the (paternal) power of desire or the (maternal) power of control, excitement, or obedience. Also, the bisexuality of the boots confirms the postulate that castration means something different in each phase: in the preoedipal phase it means giving up the sex of the other gender, whereas in the oedipal phase it means losing or renouncing one's own sexuality. If we are able to recognize both sets of desires and both renunciations/losses I believe that we are much better able to avoid the either/or controversies that characterized the classical controversies about sexuality and to stay true to the material as well.

For this woman, the mother's power had appropriated the metaphor: the aspect of the boots that would connect her to brother or father was compromised. Identification with father was blocked because he was disappointing, excluded, and sometimes dangerous, just as all subsequent attractive men seemed to be. Mother blocked the road to father not because she possessed or desired him, but because she wanted to protect and keep the daughter for herself—i.e., at a preoedipal level. In one session the patient reported reading about the Oedipus complex:

> The father is supposed to interrupt the mother-child relationship, but that was not allowed in my family. In the formula I read the child wants to stay with mother, but I was longing to have father step in. But then he didn't, so I had to find someone else. . . . What I want is not sex, it's union with the father without mother, and sex gets in the way. They say the phallus mediates the union of child and father; I say the penis gets in the way. What I want is to be little kids, those two whole little kids, and play. . . . I'm thinking of the time I made this little boat, and he insisted on floating it on the stream at the end of the field, despite my mother's vociferous protests and mine. And then it got lost, and was he in the doghouse! . . . That was the recurring thing, Daddy wants to do something irresponsible and she is protecting me. . . but maybe he was trying to show me we could have fun with something.

I said, "Maybe he was trying to show you that the boat could go off by itself, and you saw your mother was right that it couldn't, but you partly wished he had been right."

The phrase "whole little kids" referred to a memory of getting out of the bath. In this recollection, she was standing in front of the mirror and feeling great about herself, at the same time fantasizing about having alongside her another child, a boy who was a twin, also whole. Each was complete, had everything (preoedipal — being, not having, the phallus). She wanted that sort of mirroring relationship without the oedipal-sexual penis getting in the way: she and father would be alike, whole and independent — preserving the grandiosity that the rapprochement depression, and all subsequent experiences of maternal dependency and control, had deflated.

Then again, she inched up to the erotic edge of identification with father. Talking about how she and her Dad were skinny and her husband was fat, like her mother, she said, "We are both skinny, unencumbered, sexy, fleet of foot, more active than thinking." I asked, "What do you want from Dad?" She said, emphatically, "ME!" Immediately, she thought of how angry she was at a supervisor at work who had been preventing her from getting to her sessions with me by asking her to do things when it's time to leave. She had felt too guilty to stand up for herself because therapy is too self-indulgent — what she wanted from me was forbidden. This made me the forbidden "sexy man" who was outside of mother's sphere. But when I framed this conflict in terms of her fear of being unfaithful to mother, she told me that she was preoccupied with a recent incident in which she had felt spurned and ridiculed by a woman colleague with whom she was enchanted. The woman had seemed to make fun of her solicitude, discerning that the patient was infatuated with her. This experience recalled a searing childhood memory of giving her brother a present from the fair, only to have him spurn it because his friends were with him — "I was just a little girl." Not only the mother's prohibition but the humiliation of being spurned by father, brother, or me barred her way.

Again, we can note the changing positions of men and

women: the woman who plays the role of brother, the analyst who is able to be both father and mother, sometimes brother. (The woman analyst represented the father directly and not just the mother who embodied the love of the father in a "transitional" way [Ogden 1987].) As the associations made clear, the fear associated profoundly with disappointed identificatory love was not only fear of separation or mother's prohibition but of humiliation by the beloved. This humiliation, the narcissistic injury of refusal by the idealized beloved, is one key to the humiliation and punishment associated with envy of the man.

The idealized phallus of the preoedipal father can devolve on male or female. The analyst of either sex can more easily hold that position because the father of identificatory love is a volatile figure who stems from a phase in which gender is not perceived as fixed. In this case, the figure assumes many guises, including that of the brother, the idealized older woman, and the sexy man. All of these hold in common the possibility of mirroring the woman's self, allowing her to experience herself as separate, unencumbered, desiring, and having something of her own. Like the figure who possesses it, the phallus, which represents desire, also shifts in its relation to her own sexuality—sometimes it is a penis, sometimes her whole body, sometimes her own feminine sexuality.

More generally, this material shows how the symbolic identifications like "mother" and "father" establish fixed points on the internal map upon which the parents, the analyst, and the self can be imagined as movable spheres. Real objects chart their trajectory across these points, and along the axes of "masculinity" and "femininity," not in straight lines but in complex patterns. Thus we are justified in hoping that even the persistence of a gender order can allow for great change, including the possibility that mothers as well as fathers may occupy the position of representing desire.

It also follows that the phallus, the father — indeed, any love object — has more than one part to play. In our earliest experience of desire, that of identificatory love, forces that later clash seem magically reconcilable: eros and separation, idealization of the other and autonomy, are uniquely blended. And perhaps this tension, too, though hidden, also plays an important part in adult love, too, to which object love and identification, sameness and difference, both contribute. In any event, the father of separation is also an erotic father, and the child's longing to be recognized in and by this father is not only defensive or hostile to the mother. Whether it be only father or, as we hope, both mother and father who represent the first subject of desire, whoever holds this position also represents the child's love of the world. As analysts it is up to us to recognize this love in all its guises.

5 / What Angel Would Hear Me?
The Erotics of Transference

Who, if I cried, would hear me among the angelic
orders? And even if one of them suddenly
pressed me against his heart, I should dissolve in his
mightier Being. For Beauty's nothing
but beginning of Terror, we're still just able to bear,
and why we adore it so is because it serenely disdains
to destroy us. Each single angel is terrible.
And so I contain myself, and choke down the call
of depth-dark sobbing. Alas, who is there
we can make use of?

The inspiration for this essay is the opening passage of Rilke's
Duino Elegies.[1] Although Freud committed psychoanalysis to

A similar version of this essay appeared in *Psychoanalytic Inquiry* 14 (1994):535–
556. Used by permission.

1. Apologies to Stephen Spender and J. B. Leishman, whose 1939 translation I
have altered a bit in the interest of literal meaning; to wit, I have translated their
"fade in the strength of his stronger existence," as "dissolve in his mightier being,"
and "keep down my heart" I have rendered as "contain myself." In the German, it
is not a call but a mating call, *Lockruf.*

the process of demystification, it is not precisely in that spirit that I transpose the figure of the Angel from the sacred to the therapeutic. Rather, I wish to summon up that aspect of mystery which remains alive in psychoanalysis, in the erotic force of the transference. For the terrifying and powerful figure of the Angel seems to express something of the awe and danger that Freud first discovered in the relationship between Breuer and Anna O, a force equal to that of hypnosis, which tapped as yet unsuspected depths of desire (see Person 1985). Freud was later to give this force a place in the name of the transference, even though his own patient Dora seemed to flee the prospect of falling in love with him.

I will be describing the erotic transference as a transformation in which the analyst begins to assume the character of the Angel. But what is the Angel, and why is it terrible? When I first wrote this essay, I suggested that we might read in Rilke's lines an expression of the longing for recognition. After further thought, the angel seems to be not only a "recognizing angel" but the realization of Rilke's own desperate longing: to break through the barrier that separates internal and external worlds.[2] Rilke's statement at the very outset of the elegies indicates that the problem is the danger of destruction — literally, the terrible awfulness of the Angel — that this breakthrough entails. Hence, the poet has to reformulate the wish to be embraced by the Angel in the act of creation, to attain transcendence himself without the Angel — or rather, with the Angel only as a figure of identification. Leishman's commentary on the elegies (Rilke

---

2. I changed my original acceptance of Leishman's statement that the Angel embodies "perfect consciousness" partly in response to comments by Eigen. He suggests (personal communication) that we read with the idea of Imagination in mind, as the term was used by the romantic poets like Coleridge and Blake. Imagination "does not mean everything is brought from unconscious to conscious, unrealization to realization. For the work of Imagination is endless. . . . The impact of imagination as an experience creates new desire."

1939) offers notes and letters that reveal Rilke's preoccupation with expressing the internal world through the signs of the manifest, visible world, seeking "the means of expressing the suffering within us" (Rilke, cited by Leishman, p. 15). Rilke wrote that the Angel "is the creature in whom that transformation of the visible into the invisible we are performing already appears complete" (cited by Leishman, p. 87). And elsewhere he spoke of a landscape in which appearance and vision were united in the object: "In every one of them a whole inner world was exhibited, as though an angel, in whom space was included, were blind and looking into himself" (cited by Leishman, p. 10). Thus in the ninth elegy Rilke declares the poetic charge to be releasing the earth from appearance into essence, from material into ethereal being: "Earth, isn't this what you want: an invisible re-arising in us? . . . Earth invisible! What is your urgent command, if not transformation?"

One way of interpreting this movement is in terms of the wish to release and express "true self" experience (Winnicott 1960) and thus activate one's own transformational capacities.[3] The poet's awe of the Angel expresses the compelling longing

3. I use "transformation" in a sense related but not identical to Bollas's (1987) usage in his discussion of the transformational object. Bollas juxtaposes the experience of the mother as transformational object, who can alter the infant's self state, with the child's necessary disillusion and recognition that the mother is a person. I focus on later derivatives of this early state that develop in the transitional realm, which Bollas sees expressed in aesthetic experiences. I agree that the transformational wish goes on to inform the transitional experiencing, and the kind of transference manifestation I have in mind relies precisely on the metaphorical dimensions of the transitional space. This kind of transference thus presupposes that the person has gone beyond the earliest narcissistic form of transformational relation, in which one is being regulated by the other. Although it still draws some of its force from that experience of the other's power, it is now based on an awareness of certain tensions — between outside and inside, for example, or authentic feeling and inauthentic behavior. It also, as in this quotation, suggests the active role as subject of transformation, to own the capacity to create: as Eigen (1981/1993) states, "What is at stake in transitional experiencing is not mainly a self or object substitute but the creation of a symbol, of symbolizing experience itself" (p. 135).

that springs from idealization and typifies its irreducible double-sidedness: self-alienation and submission versus aspiration to a truer form of being. Searching for a way to articulate this fundamental ambiguity in our relationship to what Chasseguet-Smirgel (1985) has called "the Ideal," I was reminded of the Angel. Then, when an analysand brought me these lines and began to speak about me as the Angel, I began to sense a link between the erotic transference and this figure of the Ideal. In that analysis, a long and varied development of the Angel theme encompassed the figures of the analyst, the lover, the father, the mother, the seducer/betrayer, the redeemer. The image of the Angel could summon up a longing for unattainable transcendence and then again annihilating absorption or rejection. Above or beneath all, this was an eros of redemption — falling in love as "transfiguration," in Milner's words (1957) — that promised to release some hidden sense of meaning and connection between self and the world.

The transference erotic in which I am interested here is, like this love of the Angel, a love that can be at once heady and lamenting, elated and terrifying, hopeful and crushing. To place this notion of erotic transference in historical perspective, we must relate it to love of the Ideal, to the process of putting the other in the place of one's ego ideal, which Freud relates to love of the narcissistic type (1914) and which he discerns in the relation to both the father and the hypnotic leader (1921). The Ideal, or the Malady of the Ideal (Mallarmé, cited in Chasseguet-Smirgel 1985), is as much a feature of political as of personal life. Though respectful of its power and alert to its many meanings, Chasseguet-Smirgel (not unlike Freud) frames her views in terms of the dichotomy between rationality and irrationality, relegating the Ideal to the latter. Indeed, many critics of romanticism have emphasized the dangerous valence of the Angel's power and forsworn the temptation to search for the embodiment of holiness, knowledge, and perfection.

But other psychoanalytic writers, like Milner (1987) and more recently Eigen (1993) and Ghent (1990), have tried to integrate that search as a vital component of healing. Eigen (1993), in particular, points out that the psychoanalytic literature has "followed Freud in deciphering the pathological element in attachment to ideal states, relatively neglecting their healing aspect" (p. 74). In this vein, I propose that the desire to be recognized in one's "true self" or "spontaneous gestures," to use Winnicott's (1960) terms, fuels the creation of the Ideal and is as vital as its identificatory and libidinal aspects. A crucial premise of this notion is that insofar as the Ideal is self-generated, psychoanalysis aims at enabling a creative re-owning of it. Eigen's (1993) reframing has far-reaching import: he proposes that Freud "by a sleight of hand linked desire with ideal images without crediting the capacity" to create them (p. 103), that "one can as easily say that it is the capacity for ideal experiencing that makes eros what it is, rather than, or as well as, the reverse" (p. xix). But he also takes care to distinguish his argument from the romantic position, observing that "ideal experiencing can be perfectly hellish as well as heavenly, . . . in the service of death as well as life" (p. xix). While I want to bear this doubleness in mind, I will trace a transformation in psychoanalysis that has foregrounded the creative or heavenly aspect of the ideal, perhaps as a way to balance the closely associated destructive or demonic side.

We now confront one figure with two theoretical referents. Referring the Angel to the concept of the ego ideal assumes a different order of psychoanalytic thinking, and perhaps experiencing, than does a notion of the Ideal that includes the longing for recognition of creativity or true self experiencing.[4] The dis-

---

4. I hasten to acknowledge that true self is a highly charged, controversial concept. Insofar as it was set up by Winnicott in terms of a dichotomy with false self, it is meant to tell us something about the developmental struggle around adaptation,

tinction and relationship between these two orders may actually be crucial to understanding the double-sidedness of the Angel. To make it simpler, let us think in terms of two analytic discourses — that is, two different ways of framing the analytic experience, sometimes complementary and sometimes opposed. These two discourses roughly correspond to a parallel distinction I have described (1990, 1988) between intrapsychic and intersubjective theories, which takes off from Winnicott's (1969b) distinction between relating to the object and using it. Bollas (1989) has elaborated the intersubjective side, linking Winnicott's idea of object usage with the idea of true self, offering a distinction between interpreting the patient's unconscious and letting the patient use the analyst for true self-expression. The analyst, using her or his own countertransference awareness, aims to elicit that expression, to engage the personal aesthetic of the patient (Barbara Kane, personal communication; see Bollas 1992). I will use Bollas's formulations somewhat interchangeably with the distinction between intrapsychic and intersubjective.

In the discourse of interpretation, the erotic transference can be understood in terms of the dramatic configuration of internal objects, in which the analyst takes a part. In the discourse of object usage the erotic transference may be understood as announcing the wish to express true self feeling or the dread of expressing it (see Ghent 1990). While the interpreta-

---

as Phillips (1988) explains: whether the mother will adapt or the baby will be forced to comply precociously. The idea of compliant, reactive tendencies, designated as "false self," is congruent with the subjective experience of many individuals who are preoccupied with feeling not real, not truly alive, and to whom the idea that a vulnerable, feeling self has retreated to escape violation makes sense. If, as Phillips says, true self is an elusive idea mostly inferred by contrast to what is false, it may also be possible to say, as Steven Mitchell (1993) allows in his critique of the concept, that some experiences feel more real or alive than others, but that such experiences refer to a temporal rather than a spatial dimension. They are misrepresented if we think of a deeper "core" of self covered by a false outer layer.

tion of the erotic transference in oedipal terms (primarily as resistance) is commonplace (Hill 1994), understanding it in terms of the true self may remain elusive, mystical, or unorthodox. It may be even more unorthodox, however, to assert that the two discourses are not mutually exclusive. Eventually, I shall try to arrive at some observations about the tension between the two approaches and the way they enhance each other.

The aspect of erotic transference that I will address here has to do with the analyst as the bestower of recognition — the one who knows, or could know, the patient. To be known or recognized is immediately to experience the other's power. Omniscience can be seen as the prevailing analytic form of omnipotence (Eigen 1993). The other becomes the person who can give or withhold recognition, who can see what is hidden, can reach, conceivably even violate, the "core" of the self. This attribution of the power to know is closely bound up with erotic experience in general, but I suspect that it forms the kernel of the erotic transference. The attribution of this power in the transference may evoke awe, dread, admiration, or adoration, as well as humiliating or exhilarating submission. Once transference is "unleashed," the problem of idealization, submission, humiliation, and the corresponding resistance to those states becomes endemic.

The attitude of adoration or submission is, of course, constitutive of the relation to authority figures. The problem of submission to or compliance with authority was central to Freud's efforts to take psychoanalysis out of the sphere of manipulation, hypnosis, or persuasion and make it a rational science that appealed to the patient's own powers. Yet the subtext of Freud's central writings on the transference can be seen as the conflict between two conceptions of psychoanalysis: as submission to the physician's rational authority and as a project of liberation. Certainly, Freud believed that the analytic situation,

like any physician-patient relationship, evoked the erotic transference because of the physician's charismatic authority, and
that this evocation was dangerous. Indeed, we may read Freud
as seeking to hold in check the destructive side of the ideal.

What became more acceptable to our thought process,
since and because of Freud, was that submission to authority is
itself an erotic experience. However, understanding the erotic
experience in intersubjective terms represents an important departure from or modification of Freudian theory. Intersubjectively, submission to a powerful other may be understood as a
means, however problematic, of securing or freeing the self
and, at the same time, finding recognition. When the self is felt
to be buried or in chaos, powerless or destructive, penetration
and mastery by the powerful one serves to ward off and express
self-dissolution, to overcome abandonment (Benjamin 1980,
1988; Ghent 1990). Being pinned down, for example, becomes
a way of being held or contained; being forced to do something
serves as a supervised form of helpless abandon. The problem is
that of reconciling freedom and recognition under the inevitable condition of dependency, and the paradoxical solution is to
find freedom by surrendering one's will, to find recognition
through identification with the ideal other.

In my discussion of *Story of O* (Benjamin 1980, 1988) I have
shown how the narrative of erotic submission reveals the inner
logic of using the controlling, rational other as a means to
achieve a controlled loss of self. The condition under which the
self can transcend its boundaries and make contact with what is
outside is that the other actually transgresses and breaks these
boundaries. The condition under which the self can abandon
control is that the other takes control. The self is protected
against the terrifying void or self-dissolution that occurs when
no one is there, when merging in an equal union is felt to be impossible. This paradoxical solution can be understood in many

ways. For example, a self psychological theory (see Stolorow and Lachmann 1980) may place the emphasis on the self's fragmentation, its search for coherence and boundaries through fusion with the representation of the ideal other. Or the self may be seen as splitting off and projecting onto the other its sadistic, controlling tendencies in order to express and yet be free of them. Ghent (1990) has proposed an interpretation of sadomasochism in terms of object usage and the search for the true self experience. The sadomasochistic solution substitutes for real surrender; it is not merely defensive or shoring up the self but a covert expression of a wish. Submission, Ghent contends, is an "ever-available lookalike" for real surrender, one in which the numb, exterior false self is given up. Using the other as a containing force that facilitates surrender of the outer self and access to hidden layers of feeling can be articulated in the Winnicottian language of true and false self.

But if we return to the terms of interpretive, intrapsychic discourse, we see that the analyst as Angel can inspire a self-abnegating love, a projection of the ideal that vitiates the self. Analysis ought to offer the opportunity to reveal this self-abnegation and to detach oneself (one's libido) from the compelling object of desire. But first, of course, that desire for the powerful one is experienced in the erotic transference, quite likely heightened by the analyst's unattainability and self-control. While the erotic transference unfolds for many reasons — not least the patient's need to experience desire in a safe context — in some cases the control, order, and boundaries set by the authority figure actually excite and evoke the wish for erotic submission (see Davies 1994 on this iatrogenic effect). The analyst's promise to remain the abstinent, knowing, impenetrable physician is unconsciously rendered as an exciting, controlling, or withholding power. This unconscious rendering of the analyst's authoritative neutrality might well be seen as parallel to the articulation of

disinterestedness by the masters in *Story of O:* "We do this not for
our pleasure but for your enlightenment." The very aloofness of
the analyst may be registered as the negative current that need
only make contact with the patient's positive charge to complete
the circuit of desire.

For Freud, the infiltration of love by power, as well as the
representation of the analyst's knowledge in the unconscious
language of erotic power, was unavoidable. The route to freedom must necessarily pass through the dangerous straits of subjection. Liberation from the slavish love of power could be
effected only by summoning up the powerful figures and making the erotic impulses manifest, "for when all is said and done,
it is impossible to destroy anyone in absentia, in effigy" (1912a,
p. 108). The aim of detachment from the early love is to enable
the patient to "gain free command over a function which is of
such inestimable importance to her" (1915b, p. 169). Corresponding to this valorizing of the patient's mental freedom,
Freud placed increasing value on the freedom of association
within the analytic process.

In the last of his series of "Recommendations to Physicians," his "Observations on Transference-Love," (1915b),
Freud resumed the discussion of the physician's power to evoke
the patient's idealizing love. He again argued that transference
love must be allowed free rein, so that the patient's resistance to
giving it up might be truly worked through and that it might be
renounced because of insight rather than coercion. He sounded
a reprise of his earlier analysis of the transference dynamics as
a conflict of opposing forces, one that aligned the "the doctor
and the patient" with the oppositions "between intellect and
instinctual life, between understanding and seeking to act"
(1912a, p. 108). Like Odysseus tied to the mast, the analyst must
resist the patient's effort to assert "her irresistibility, to destroy
the physicians's authority by bringing him down to the level of

the lover" (1915b, p. 163). Of course, this interpretation of the patient's attempt to "bring down" authority has a distinctly pejorative meaning for Freud, one that emphasizes the aspect of resistance rather than the underlying wish to be known. (And the associated stance, then and now, is to exculpate the doctor for succumbing to temptation and blame the patient for the seduction.) Still, the analyst's self-mastery would become the basis for the patient's freedom: "She has to learn from him to overcome the pleasure principle . . . to achieve this overcoming of herself . . . to acquire that extra piece of mental freedom that distinguishes conscious mental activity" (1915b, p. 170).

The idea is that the resolution of the erotic transference consists in the patient's identification with the self-mastering analyst. Rather than loving him as an object, she must, in the axiomatic move from love to identification, put him in the place of her ego ideal. The analyst's power to understand has been redistributed; no longer magical, it is now comprehensible and accessible. This, at least, is the outcome Freud envisioned, as if in direct response to Kant's query in "What is Enlightenment?": how it is possible to work gradually through tutelage to freedom in self-mastery?

But the difficulty in Freud's position (a problem Ferenczi first recognized and struggled with in depth) was the distance it established between analyst and patient, each of whom represented only one side in the struggle between reason and instinct. This polarization persists despite Freud's emphasis on self-analysis and awareness of authority, for it is lodged in the discourse of illness, the configurations of female patient and male doctor. What is missing, as from so many of Freud's formulations, is a certain kind of recognition by the analyst of *his* self in the patient's struggle; identification is a one-way street (see Kristeva 1987). The analyst is like a chemist working with "highly explosive forces" (1915b, p. 170). Thus the analyst's

authority is never fully dissolved; the patient can take the analyst as model, but the model itself is not questioned except
in defiance. Already idealized for his knowledge and power—
his power to know her—the analyst is now internalized in the
relationship of knowledge as power over self, a practice in the
dominion of self whose meaning Foucault (1980) has made un-
forgettably problematic.

Although it has been pointed out often enough that the
model in his transference recommendations presumes the relation of male doctor to female hysteric, Freud himself never
wrote a case story that followed the heterosexual scenario of
patient-doctor love except for the one involving Breuer and
Anna O. Freud's most famous female case studies involved
women who would not submit to the transference, who refused
the one-sided offer of identification, and who, like Dora and the
unnamed homosexual woman, defied the analyst. If Freud offers
an exemplification of this model of internalization, in which the
patient takes the beloved analyst as ego ideal, it is probably in the
relationship between training analyst and analysand/student, a
man-to-man model. Of course, given Freud's encouragement of
female disciples (his daughter, above all), the relationship of
tutelage did not always devolve upon men or actually fall along
male-female gender lines, but it did remain a masculine relationship ("on this point you're more masculine than feminine"). And
it seems that the idealized and loving transference that Freud
made paradigmatic lay in that homoerotic master-disciple relationship. This erotic paradigm and its perpetuation in the transference to Freud's theory continue to be a pervasive effect in the
psychoanalytic world. Freud's own reflections (1921) on the
group's submission to the ideal authority figure and hypnosis,
which link the ego ideal to the preoedipal father, point to this
transference. There he related the process of putting the charis-

matic figure in the place of the ego ideal to the little boy's tendency to idealize his father. Love for the analyst as the representative of knowledge/power would thus expectably appear at least as frequently in the homoerotic transference as in the heterosexual one.

It is only a short step from being in love to hypnosis, Freud contended, and his understanding of the transference love aimed to acknowledge but finally overcome the power common to both. For him, the key to overcoming the dangers of this power lay in identification, in a form of tutelage that sustains authority by passing it on, as in the oedipal promise of becoming like father. But the factor that determines whether the path of identification with the ideal ends in self-respect or in submission, as I have pointed out regarding the father-child relationship (Benjamin 1986, 1988), is whether the identification and the recognition are in some sense mutual: the father must say not only, "You can become like me," but also, "I was once like you and I remember how that feels." Identificatory love, the force that underlies the homoerotic transference, may culminate in submission or in the inheritance of power, sometimes even in an inheritance that allows the possibility of self-determination. Certainly, without the father/analyst's loving recognition, the project of self-governance cannot be freed from the axis of submission and defiance. In the analytic situation, more is required to dissolve the erotic idealization than the confrontation with the transference; the analyst's countertransference communication, unconscious and conscious, is equally important. The recognition in the countertransference is what transforms the process from internalization to collaboration.

Thus, the theoretical step taken by psychoanalytic thought subsequent to Freud is that the analyst's countertransference recognition — empathy, attunement, and identification with the patient—is as decisive for change as is the modeling of self-knowledge and self-mastery through the interpretation of unconscious forces. It is this step, I suggest, that modifies the link between knowledge and power that critics of psychoanalysis, such as Foucault, saw as indissoluble. It begins to open the possibility of dissolving love of authority rather than merely internalizing it. In light of this and other related changes in our analytic stance, what becomes of our understanding of the erotic transference?

As the world outside psychoanalysis has changed, an understanding has emerged that has disentangled the need for the father from the need for authority and has separated the figure of analyst from the figure of the father. The father/analyst does not represent the only knower, the only ego ideal, the only form of power. Phallic penetration is not the unquestioned metaphor of knowledge. And what the father provides is no longer represented primarily in terms of power. These changes reflect both a changed external reality and the internal evolution of psychoanalysis; these, in turn, have led to a greater emphasis on the transference to the mother and on mutuality in the transference (Aron 1994). The analyst's felt identification with the patient forms much of the basis for her or his awareness, creating the sense of a cooperative exploration of human experience. Thus the notion of the erotic transference as the site of the struggle between analyst and patient against the instincts, in which the analyst represents simply the idealized knower and figure of power, seems antiquated. And this development raises further interrelated questions: how does the new emphasis on the intersubjective relationship of recognition between analyst and patient change the view of erotic transference? And how does the maternal character of the analytic activity change the transference eroticism—how would the maternal Angel differ from the paternal one, and what alternate route to freedom would the mother figure offer?

The shift to a focus on the mother was indisputably linked to a change in the metaphors of knowing and love in psychoanalysis, to an emphasis on the relationship between two subjects, and to the evolution of the discourse of object usage rather than interpretation. The images, narratives, and harbingers of the maternal transference may be different, as may be some of the developmental needs that stimulate them. But, I should emphasize caution, the distinction between paternal and maternal reflects the many-layered sediments of culture; the privileged relation of the maternal transference to object usage relies on certain culturally constituted conventional gender pairings, which are, I hope, changing. The use of the figures "mother" and "father" refers not to biologically ordained categories but to theoretical ideal types, which derive from historically lived cultural experience and enter the psyche as ideal representations, sometimes disjunctive and sometimes overlapping with our individual experience. It is important not to conflate these ideal types with concrete reality, even if we cannot do without them in our theory.

Because this typography is so thoroughly entrenched in our language and culture, the formulation of gender dualism to express complementary relationships corresponds to the metaphors of our psychic experience; we may use these metaphors while recognizing them to be neither facts of nature nor without contradiction (Dimen 1991). But uninformed by this awareness, metaphors harden into stereotypes that conceal more than they reveal. The uncritical acceptance of the association of the maternal with holding has led unwittingly to idealized notions of therapeutic reparation, founded in magical beliefs about maternal power. The emphasis on maternal reparation may over-shadow woman's struggle to become a desiring subject, to appropriate nonmaternal aspects emphasized in the intrapsychic discourse of sex and aggression.

On the one hand, then, I want to make use of a grid that aligns masculinity and femininity with intrapsychic and inter-subjective categories, in which the maternal experience of holding and containment forms a counterpoint to the image of phallic penetration (see Benjamin 1988). But on the other hand, I want to challenge that grid on the grounds that even in our gender-polarized world the figures of mother and father are more multiple and mixed up, less identical with femininity and masculinity, than the grid allows. I want to make it clear that both masculinity and femininity are registered in the psycho-sexual symbolic language as well as in the intersubjective dis-course of space. So, for example, to take up aspects of the maternal transference related to containment does not oblige us to dispense with aspects of idealization or the dread of surrender that have previously been formulated in the intrapsychic discourse of bodily symbolism. I hope to make a double-edged point here: that the categorical distinction between phallic fa-ther and containing mother is metaphorically useful to capture unconscious identifications, and that for precisely that reason these pairings are the proper object of our analysis. They can and should be transcended in some relationships, destabilized and revealed to be contradictory in others.

I have tried to suggest that the paternal erotic transference may often be less oedipal than was previously thought. The paternal erotic transference evoked in the figure of the Angel may well refer more to the dyadic preoedipal father of identi-ficatory love and the ego ideal than to the romantically con-ceived, heterosexual father presumed in the scenario of male doctor and female hysteric. Nonetheless, the eroticism of the paternal transference is evoked by the fantasy of the analyst's omniscience. The relationship to the ideal in this form may be homoerotic or heteroerotic, but the form of authority is still read as masculine, and so is less likely to devolve on female analysts, or perhaps less likely to be noticed when it does. Person (1985; 1988) has contended that the experience of loving someone powerful who is the self's ideal is far more likely to be directed toward male analysts by women than toward female analysts by men. When women are powerful, they are not commonly imbued with eroticism and do not evoke a parallel experience of the Ideal. Maternal power, in this logic, is too much about dependency (anal control), too little about the excitement of identifying with someone powerful, to inspire a romantic erotic transference.

But this viewpoint also seems to accept without challenge the desexualization and de-eroticization of the mother in our culture, and perhaps proclaims as absent what is merely excluded from conscious representation (see Irigaray 1991a), perhaps out of fear or humiliation (Chasseguet-Smirgel 1976). The search for the Angel in maternal garb may help to articulate hitherto unarticulated, unconscious aspects of erotic experience. If so, we must then speculate about how the maternal erotic transference might differ from that directed to the father/analyst of power/knowledge. We might discern a different metaphor for the maternal form of knowledge as power, thereby casting a different slant on the Angel, the ideal, and the love of knowledge as power. Contesting the paternal-phallic idea of the analyst who is idealized as the "one supposed to know" (in Lacan's famous formulation) is the idea of the analyst as "the one who knows *me*."[5] This contrast coincides with the typical

5. Lacan's idea of "the subject supposed to know" links knowledge to omnipotence, setting up the transference as an encounter with the impossibility of such

gender pairings: masculine/universal versus feminine/particular, masculine/abstract versus feminine/personal. The one who empathically understands, who is emotionally attuned to me, is associated with maternal functions of holding, containing, attuning. This knowing, like the paternal erotic, is also subject to idealization and evokes longings for unattainable fulfillment.

The historical shift to maternal imagery in psychoanalysis has not only been associated with the idea of holding or containing rather than penetrating with insight; more specifically, this emphasis has been closely allied with another metaphor of analysis as the creation of a space. It is a space in which two subjectivities must necessarily interact so that one subjectivity can be explored in detail.[6] It includes many aspects of preverbal dialogue associated with mother-infant interaction — awareness of the other person's affect, the sense of having an impact, the contours of intensity, the kinetic timing, the choreography of turning toward and away from the other — all of which can be represented internally in presymbolic form as interaction schemas (Beebe and Lachmann 1988). These schemas form the basis of our expectation of being close or distant, matched and

---

knowledge. Kristeva (1987), however, working out of Lacanian theory, argues against this notion as the sole basis of the transference and arrives at a similar critique of the tyranny of the concept of idealization that excludes the aspect of "countertransference as identification."

6. But the intersubjective orientation has several branches, with quite different views of the analyst's provision with different gender connotations: the position of self psychology emphasizes empathy and attunement (see Atwood and Stolorow 1984), whereas the "relational-conflict" (S. Mitchell 1988) and social-constructivist views (Hoffman 1991), which place greater emphasis on confrontation with the separate reality of the analyst, have masculine connotations of emphasizing boundaries and separation. Furthermore, there are significant differences in the interpretation of interaction, which may be seen as intrapsychic in content though occurring between two distinct subjects. If we were to say that the analyst's countertransference identification with the patient distinguishes the intersubjective position from the opposing view that the analyst controls himself and holds fast to the mast of reality in order to carry the patient through the treacherous waters of the transference, the differences within the position would lie in what aspects of the identification are utilized and who is seen as adapting to whom.

met, or violated and impinged upon. Further, the mutual gazing, gesturing, and vocalizing in this interaction form a kind of erotic dance which is a fundament of the mutual attunement and pleasure of adult sexuality as well. This presymbolic but representable aspect of eroticism is part of the unconscious communication in the analytic situation as well.

The world of presymbolic representation resonates with the use of spatial metaphors invoked by Winnicott and his followers: spatial metaphors are linked not only to the idea of transitional experiencing but also to that of being alone in the presence of the other (which Sander [1983] has called "open space"), as well as to the idea of impingement versus nonintrusiveness. I have observed that the unfolding of woman's desire has been linked to images of such aloneness, an intersubjective space that allows the self to come alive (Benjamin 1986, 1988). In the solitude provided by the other the subject has a space to become absorbed with internal rhythms rather than reacting to the outside; this space is a counterpoint to the image of phallic penetration in the erotic experience of being known. This experience in the transference has its countertransference correlate, in which the analyst imagines her- or himself sharing with the patient a similar state of intense absorption and receptivity, immersed in a flow of material without the need to actively interpret or organize or inject her- or himself. A broadened category of transference erotics might be able to gather up these aspects of the analytic situation and their representation in metaphor. An expanded notion of eroticism might allow us to identify the maternal erotic transference precisely in those aspects that do not form a mirror image of the paternal erotic transference.[7]

7. Eigen (1993) has set up a somewhat different distinction between the images of the face and the experience of the breath that relate to ideal images in contrast to the libidinal aspects of instinctual images. Along these lines I suggest that the mother's face often comes to represent the primordial experience of beauty, and

But this association of maternal holding with spatial metaphors does not tell the whole story. For the experience of the
mother Angel has the double-sidedness of all idealization, self-
diminution as well as self-expression. Furthermore, the container mother figure can be understood in the psychosexual
symbolic language of interpretative discourse as well as in the
intersubjective discourse of object usage. It is also embodied,
and it does contain that which Winnicott (1969b), in a venture
into naturalism, attributed to the masculine side: "the drive
element" as opposed to "BEING," which is associated with the
"pure, uncontaminated female element." We may further object to this grid on the grounds that with the advent of symbolic
functioning, previous presymbolic experience becomes blended
with the symbolic language of the body, which also incorporates
the presymbolic concrete body experiences of suckling, holding, excreting, etc. The mother can be the "anal controlling,
phallic mother" or a "tantalizing breast mother" who is longed
for but unattainable, and both of these can stimulate fantasies of
erotic submission, regardless of the analyst's sex. The elision
from maternal breast to paternal penis, as Klein pointed out
early on, leads to many condensations of maternal and paternal
attributes. And this slippage is intensified by the culturally contingent mediations that ensue as maternal and paternal are further differentiated and cross-referenced.

An implicit assumption in relational theory — that only the
mother is associated with the early sensuality, as well as the early
gazing and play, of infancy — underlies the affiliation between
the imagined maternal/feminine and experiences described by

---

that it is an intersubjective experience: beauty belongs to the beloved who returns
the gaze, in whose eyes we see the sun. But in this first beauty, in the mutual gaze,
also lies the beginning of terror — awe, idealization, overstimulation, violation,
loss.

intersubjective theory. But does this association of the maternal with the preverbal body (see Chapter 3) misattribute to mother what may belong to infancy itself (Eigen 1993)? Would the association of the maternal with the intersubjective simply introduce a mass of contradictions? Then again, can these contradictions be avoided as long as we use the intrapsychic metaphors of the body, which are necessarily gendered, and so throw into question the apparent gender neutrality of references to potential space? The kinship between the analytic metaphors of containing mental products and of holding the baby, the spatial metaphors of the inside of the maternal body, refer to profoundly important fantasies. It is no accident that the development of maternal metaphors accompanied the exploration of preverbal, spatial, and kinetic representation. On the one hand, then, we do not wish to hypostatize a split between the intersubjective and the intrapsychic perspectives along gender lines. On the other hand, we are required to recognize that because the gender split is anchored in collective fantasy, it necessarily returns, often unnoticed, in our theoretical formulations and in transference and countertransference (Dimen 1991). What we might adapt from Winnicott's perspective is the possibility of seeing these gender alignments as transitional categories, and we might then find in the intersubjective space of psychoanalysis a freedom to move through or around the categories, to play with these fantasies.

Bearing in mind these complexities, the exploration of the maternal transferences will reveal aspects of both intrapsychic and intersubjective dimensions. In an article on the maternal erotic transference, Welles and Wrye (1991) discuss the erotic horror of experiencing in fantasy the body of the mother/therapist, as well as the wish to make a mess and have the toilet/container/mother/therapist hold and not flush away all the bits the patient presents. A woman patient had the sensation of an involuntary bowel movement running down her leg. She had the fantasy that if she ever let go in vaginal orgasm there would be a giant explosive bowel movement.

The authors' use of the term *maternal erotic transference* is refreshing. The term refers not to romantic oedipal idealization of the mother/analyst (which would be explicitly homosexual), but rather to passionate longing for the sensual pregenital mother — sometimes a breast mother and sometimes an anal mother. The emphasis on pregenital polymorphous strivings and their association with feelings of excitement and longing seems to be a useful return to psychosexual theory, thereby enlarging our notion of erotic transference, freeing it from the phallic monism (Chasseguet-Smirgel 1976) assumed in our heterosexual/genital/oedipal model of development, and reopening the importance of bisexuality.

Although it is not their central concern, the authors mention the problem of the patient's false self, a performing, precociously intellectual self that has covered over the passionate longing for the mother and for immersion in her body. Grasping this longing constitutes a crucial extension of our thinking about the part eroticism plays in relation to true-self emergence, especially in women. We can view Welles and Wrye's description of pregenital bodily experiences through the lens of Ghent's (1990) discussion of related imagery as expressing the wish for surrender. Welles and Wrye's idea that "erotic horror" signals the emergence of bodily fantasy in the maternal erotic transference may be related to Ghent's idea of the dread that signals the emergence of surrender. Ghent describes an incident in which the patient, experiencing in the transference relationship a momentary "glimpse of a nascent lovable self" that was about to be discovered by the analyst, perverted that perception into a violent fantasy of penetration, masochistic exposure, and self-abuse.[8] Although "erotic horror" may take somewhat different forms in the maternal and paternal transference, both forms may serve the function of signaling threat to a vulnerable self that longs for surrender.

In sum, the maternal figure can be as idealized or as dominated by psychosexual imagery as can the paternal figure, even though the primary intersubjectivity of direct, presymbolic recognition has been associated in our theory with the maternal. Our common mental life and our theory have provided us with both a maternal and a paternal Ideal — the two faces of the Angel. Each face has two sides, reflecting the double possibility of recognition or idealization, and each can be construed in terms of both analytic discourses. It has largely been the expansion of our theory in the maternal direction that has allowed us to articulate the side of intersubjectivity, of recognition, and of the transitional aspects of the analytic space. But in this context, we need to be aware that the same kind of idealization that crept into Freud's original formulations of the neutral, interpreting physician analyst might be embedded in formulations of the analyst's role as tender of the intersubjective. We are obliged to consider that the lure of the Angel can be as dangerous in the maternal countertransference as in the paternal, holding out the hope of perfect reparation and denying the Angel's annihilating aspects. These issues will draw us into future revisions of our ideas about transference and gender. With these caveats

8. The main problem in Ghent's account is unclarity about the necessity of resistance as well as of the dissolving of idealization through the elements of aggression and ruthlessness. The patient's masochism in the face of an earlier "surrender" to vulnerability may reflect an inability to mobilize necessary protection of the "inviolable core," to make use of the kind of negation that can prevent a return to compliance, this time in the form of submission to "cure." Recognition of negativity in relation to the analyst needs to be factored in as a condition of letting go, vital to the analysand's creativity and sense of power.

in mind, let us devote more attention to the transference erotics of the maternal figure.

I shall briefly illustrate clinically the imagery of maternal erotic transference both in the tensions around idealization/submission/longing related to the maternal body, and in the underlying wish to find through recognition the potential space of true-self discovery. I shall first describe an analytic sequence in relation to the maternal figure to illustrate a transition from achieving abandon and release by submission (to a phallic maternal force) toward a mode of transitional experiencing in which there is an experience of no coercion, freedom and solitude, contact with the core of the self.

This woman's early relationship to an overstimulating, hovering mother presented issues addressed by both psychoanalytic discourses — the psychosexual elements and the intersubjective elements in the fantasy of submission. Her experience typified the situation that Ghent (1990) sees as frequently formative in masochism: having been subjected to consistent impingement and having developed a reactive self, the woman sought some external power that would force or seduce her into giving up the deadening, reactive "superstructure" so that she might be known, or found. The real break from this pattern emerged in an experience of spatial awareness, a recapturing of the sense of self in solitude inside the analytic session.

The early part of the treatment was characterized by the patient's many efforts to get the analyst to force her or tell her what to do, to act "more stimulating." Following this period, she began to describe the frantic autoerotic activities in which she had engaged from early childhood, seeking to spend herself, to be released, to sustain increasingly long moments of orgasm in which consciousness was obliterated. These experiences were associated with fantasies that her body was distorted and monstrous, but also with dreams containing alienated images of the maternal body as vacuum cleaner or rotting melon. In one session she described in detail her childhood and adult sexual practices, recounting her wish to be out of control and her method of dividing herself into the voice of the master and the one who had to do what the master said. As a child she had devised a form of masturbation in which the master, whom she now recognized as mother, would say, "You must take this!" No matter how intense the stimulation, she must and would comply. She closed by saying that she could not open up to anyone but that inner voice and that the analyst was in the camp of everyone who is outside.

The next session began with a long, uncharacteristic silence. This was perhaps the first such beginning. Finally, the patient remarked on a patch of light thrown by the window onto the wall she was facing, perhaps suggesting water or trees. She had had a dream that included the words, "It was so big and so small." With "It" she associated

> Vagina. Some epic thing I had gone through. I also think of me as "It" — and It was something beyond my grasp, something about me and the rest of the world. That little patch of light. As a kid I would go to a special spot by the river, walk through those trees alone, listen to my own thoughts, hear myself, find some peace . . . something about illusion and fantasy and substance. . . . My mother had no peace, ever. It was a long walk to get to that spot . . . or going to all kinds of extremes with myself, to within myself . . . some private place. I would go to the river, there was a place, a clearing in the trees, I would sing "Somewhere Over the Rainbow." . . . It was my private escape where I didn't have to mirror or reflect the ones around me, a peaceful place equivalent to the place of orgasm — two places where no one else is there, where I can feel myself, suck in the air and hold it, hold my own breath.

A few months later she had a dream about a woman with

long golden hair who ferries people on a boat to paradise, and she reflected that she herself would like to have that job. She associated: "Blue and water represents the infinite, peaceful space, let go of control. Paradise is a place where I wouldn't be invaded, so maybe my consciousness has created this place so I wouldn't be invaded. It's like in the most ultimate climax sexually, I lose myself. It can also be self-destructive, like when speed hits your bloodstream, escape. I am so far outside and within myself, I can't be invaded. Certain spots in nature, desert, wind, some private space nobody else can take away." She juxtaposed this experience with the man with the powerful penis, who takes her away, outside herself, into abandon and oblivion. And she remembered a wonderful nursery school teacher with long blonde hair, a teacher who had let her be and made her feel accepted, and whom she had visited after the teacher had had a baby, watching for the first time a baby being breast-fed.

These maternal images of abandon to a deep place in the self and to transitional experiencing, which are expressed as much in relation to nature as to others, are set against images of submissive abandon to both maternal and masculine phallic forces. The erotic transference figure here seems to be an almost literal golden-haired Angel who contains and carries across the water — a role that the patient can imagine for herself. She invokes an eroticism of opening to inner-body discovery as well as of sucking at the breast and being carried in mother's body. There is also a hint of something else: the possible association of the water crossing with death as a kind of ultimate self-dissolution in surrender. The association between dissolution of false self and a discovery of a space of freedom in solitude may be important elements in the erotic transference. Eigen in the illuminating "Winnicott's Area of Freedom" (1993), talks of Winnicott's patient who, "buried in an image of goodness," became able to "taste the freedom that recognition of lack provides . . . to treasure the space made possible by real absence, a gap not stuffed by falseness" (p. 146). The patient here used the nonimpingement of the analytic space to facilitate a transition from an eroticism of force and submission to one of free surrender, from empty goodness to good emptiness.

Another case illustrates the interweaving of maternal psychosexual themes and intersubjective ones, specifically the messing and smearing associated with the anal mother combined with the fantasy of being recognized and understood. A patient confessed that her private names for me were "shrinky-poo" and, through a later derivation, "stinky-poo," The Bad Smell. Often she had expressed fear of making a mess on the couch, and on this occasion she associated this fear with making a stink about my leaving on vacation. She fervently hoped that I would understand how, within the privacy of her own self, these names were "very fondly meant — fond and grumpy." The feeling of dread at making a mess was related to the surrender, the letting go, symbolized by the act of revelation. Taking the pet names out of the body/diaper into the outer space between us and exposing herself would make what was good bad, as it once had. The wish was that the transitional space of communication might transform this good/badness into shared understanding of the "fond meaning," the wish for love.

The dread might be more deeply related to this wish to be discovered as a lovable self, which equated the explicit sexual fantasies with making a mess (see Milner 1952). What she deliberately held back in the last session before vacation, when she had wanted to make the "stink," was her feeling of sexual attraction to me. The expression of the erotic transference would have meant letting go, risking disclosure of her greedy wish to hold onto me, a wish that had to be both wonderful and dreadful. At the same time, though, making me the one who "stinks" made me into the engulfing maternal body who refuses to allow her daughter's independence. This was the "grumpy" side, referring to the threat to her separation posed by me as the tantalizing object. She wanted me to accept her mess and her desire but was afraid that she might therefore have to accept mine, hence The Bad Smell. In this light, did her stated wish to be both fond and grumpy, apparently a reparative gesture of accepted ambivalence, not also express the taming of a more violent urge to mix it up with me sexually and aggressively, to make poo of me, to run from my overpowering desirability?

Then again, the vision of "poo" as good love is associated with a state of beatitude, a kind of redemption in which all is goodness, even badness. The shrinky-poo is a version of the adored Angel, whose strength guarantees the freedom to turn mother into warm mush and then back again into a sexually idealized body, the paradise where everything is beauty — from hell to heaven in the blink of an eye. With the idealization comes humiliation and a sense of the object's unattainability, as well as the fear of being cast out of paradise.

In yet another way, the connection between a longing to let go and the making of a mess is associated with surrender. Dreams of going to the analyst as going to the toilet are common, but a true letting go of everything inside is not so easily attained. All-out, body-giving, surrendering defecation or urination is for some people the very image of abandon, but it is checked by the dread of being destructive, too much for the other to bear, and by the fear of madness, merging, and self-dissolution (Milner 1957).

A final example may serve to illustrate the ambiguity of our categories of maternal and paternal eroticism, while yet affirming the expanded notion of transference erotics that maternal imagery has lent us. This patient's dream, in which the erotic partner was a man, followed many associations about women. It came after a long period of anxiety about lying down and about free association. The patient felt that to let go and say whatever came to her mind would be crazy. Immediately prior to this dream she began a session by being able to express the wish, "Don't go!" This utterance was prompted by material in the preceding hour: she had been musing about having a crush on a woman but then becoming revulsed, about wanting so much and then becoming disillusioned, and this made her think of her mother. "I'm afraid you'll be revulsed," she said. "I want to say, 'Don't go away, don't go away!'" The next time she stated that she felt as though she had taken a leap into something and survived. Telling everything that was in her head, saying, "Don't go away!" felt wonderful. She reported a dream about a young man, a kind of beat (as in beatitude) poet: "We are swimming in very clear water near the shore, it's tropical, the kind of water that you scuba dive in. There is a world underneath the surface of coral and shapes, you could see everything. We were swimming naked and then lying on the shore, extremely erotic, holding each other, stroking each other. I was feeling so happily clean, I could do anything I wanted, licking and sucking." She remembered that before they could have intercourse, they were interrupted. She spoke of the redemptive experience, the world underneath water that you get to in scuba diving, "a wonderful, wonderful world, such a relief to get to it, very quiet. You could never replicate it, you have to be there — how like *here* that is."

The erotically charged transitional state made the analytic space into an "ideal" container — the beautiful waters — in which the inner world of the self could be found. The waters of the self and the waters of the analytic space flowed into each other, the outer and inner space met in the in-between that was the site of an inward journey. What was found in this space was also created — the corals and shapes were both inside and outside. The flowing of the idealization out onto the analyst and the analytic space makes for Paradise, a space of self-discovery. The analysand has the experience of floating on the couch. What I am describing is an aspect of what Eigen (1993) calls the area of freedom, "between aloneness and intersubjective aliveness." The core of self feels freed of the burden of self-protection, at once known and yet left alone, supported without gravity in a space I would call "zero coercion."

The freedom from internal and external constraint of the object, floating in the reflection of the other's knowledge, which need not be distinguished from self's knowledge, informs the erotics of the intersubjective space. This experience of being known generates a profound sense of love, but it leans more toward the idealization of the analysis than toward the idealization of the analyst as sexual love object. Though both may appear in the same analysis, this erotics of transference does differ from the well-known erotic transference, the genitally charged passion of falling in love with the analyst, from that form of urgent desire that involves possession and being "possessed." Still, it is a romantic fantasy nonetheless, subject to the vicissitudes of the Ideal, to delight and disappointment. Hidden behind the better-known erotic transference, the fantasy of recognition, the desire to be known, has to find a place; opening up possibilities in the transitional area and in loving the other, in self-knowledge and self-expression, it must find a way to survive outside paradise, between heaven and hell.

For every paradise has its fall, every ideal its confrontation with reality. In the working through of transference, the Angel must fall — must become demonic or lose her/his powers, must be recognized as human, imperfect — but the analytic relationship must survive, enriched. For this analysand, the Angel became the blue-robed Madonna of Renaissance painting, but then turned into a tantalizer, seducer, and destroyer: "The Blue Angel." The desire to be destroyed, the dread/terror/joy of dissolution, alternated with horror and fear. The dream of the beautiful waters was swiftly followed by dreams of the toilet — one that is not always there when it is most urgently needed. Sometimes the transference became viscous and suffocating, heavy with the sheer effort to suppress the dread of flying off into space, the terror of dissolution in the analyst's power. The conviction of being lovable alternated with profound fears of seduction and rejection or exclusion. In the heady altitude of high transference love, the smallest gesture can portend the fall. Both analyst and analysand may experience a magnified volatility of transitional space, which now becomes an unbearable lightness, permitting a frightening susceptibility to metaphors that carry the magnetic charge of the Ideal.

This susceptibility, the idealization of the analyst as Angel, is not only tempered by falling and disillusion, by awareness of destructiveness or humiliation, not only disappointed and dispelled. Rather, the lightness is countered by what feels substantial and grounded, the shared (re)experiencing of pain and loss — the mourning for what was lost as well as for that which can never be. In that experience of pain lies a different kind of aliveness, a different sense of being at one with ourselves. The dissolution of the idealization in these transference erotics may parallel what Winnicott said about the transitional space: it is not internalized as structure but rather becomes distributed in creative and cultural activity. I suggest that the resolution of this erotic transference to the analyst who engenders that space is neither through internalization as ego ideal (although that may still pertain to other aspects of the analyst) nor only through giving up the Ideal (although that, too, is vital). In being given up as "the real thing, out there" the Ideal must be preserved as an inner capacity for certain states of concentrated being.

This giving up/preserving resolution is constituted by the analysand's knowledge of her or his own creativity, her or his ability to use the object and use the space, which begins to extend outward to experiences of communication and solitude, play and passion, beyond the couch. The analyst's recognition facilitates a developing confidence in the real feeling of freedom and aliveness that accompanies the "spontaneous gesture," the emergent "force of idiom" that Bollas (1989) describes. In this sense, Freud's notion that through the playground of the erotic transference the patient would come to be in charge of her own passion remains pertinent; what has changed and grown are the meanings of transference as "playground" and of owning one's passion: "that extra piece of mental freedom."

6 / Sympathy for the Devil: Notes on Sexuality and Aggression, with Special Reference to Pornography

The occasion for these remarks was a conference on pornography, which led me to speculate about the excitement associated with sadistic fantasies and images of sexual violation. Viewing a number of pornographic works, the participants in the conference were compelled to conclude that their awareness of sexual objectification and degradation, even their revulsion, did not exclude fascination and excitement. Indeed, any observers who can tolerate the conflict may note with dismay their own excited responses to fantasies or images of acts that they know would in reality be distasteful, perhaps frightening or even traumatic. The same sexual fantasy may at one moment seem to incarnate some exciting aspect of otherness, at another appear terrifying, at yet another appear only as degrading repetition. The conflict that pornography inspires actually pertains to the realm of sexual fantasy as a whole: Pornography is a particularly sharp form of the disjunction between fantasy and reality, be-

An early version of this essay was presented at the conference on Pornography and Representation, Center for the Psychological Study of the Arts, SUNY-Buffalo, May 1987.

tween symbolic representations and real interaction. My interest in this essay was therefore to reach some understanding, beyond the mundane, about this disjunction between sexual fantasy and reality. Such an exploration must necessarily try to illuminate the sadistic component of sexual fantasy and thus reveal something about how aggression becomes implicated in sexuality.

The fact that the sources of sexual excitement in fantasy diverge so widely from the sources in real interaction does not mean, as common wisdom has it, that fantasy is privileged to reveal the truth concealed by outer reality. Such a notion of truth vastly oversimplifies the complicated relationship of wish, fantasy, and reality. It implies that reality "is," that it has one truth, and that this truth can be known apart from the complex process of psychic representation. For example, some feminist opponents of pornography say that its contents expose the truth about "the male compulsion to dominate and destroy that is the source of sexual pleasure for men" (Dworkin 1980, p. 289). Not only does this stance imply the existence of an essential masculine nature, which the lifting of cultural repression would expose, it also equates the acts portrayed in pornography with what all men really wish for in their sexual life. It further implies that such wishes are simply what they appear to be: they do not represent any other motives or processes beyond themselves; they are what they are.

Of course, Dworkin's statement also implies that violence, transgression, abomination — all the heterogeneous elements (Bataille 1985) that the Angel in the House declares to be anathema — are alien to and absent from women. Women's participation in sexual domination, if not explained away as the result of coercion, would mean that women's nature is as pornography portrays it: submissive, violated. And this conclusion is indeed problematic for feminists. If men inevitably are what they are, then how can women not be what they are?

The conventional association of femininity with submission is a "truth" to be confronted, and the most serious of the feminists against pornography, Catherine MacKinnon, has conceded this point. Although her analysis is rather simple, MacKinnon (1987) has courageously insisted that women do experience sexual pleasure under the current conditions of abuse and "dehumanization"; they are not simply abused against their will. She grants that for women "subordination is sexualized, the way that dominance is for the male, as pleasure as well as gender identity, as femininity." MacKinnon argues with those who would salvage sex by freeing it from the onus of violence: "Violence is sex when it is practiced as sex." Hence "if violation of the powerless is part of what is sexy about sex," we must take another look at sexuality (pp. 5–8).

But MacKinnon does not really take a look at sexuality. She relies on such simple notions as the premise that gender psychology works through "social defining" of men and women. She does not try to unlock the mystery of what makes violation and powerlessness exciting; of how the hierarchy of gender insinuates itself into or "discursively constructs" (Martin 1982; Butler 1990) sexual pleasure; of how violence can be experienced and practiced as sex. Instead she flattens the most difficult problem into the proposition that "violence *is* sex." Because men dominate, they are able to use sexuality as a means of perpetuating control. What sexuality "is," and why it can be instrumentalized, remain mysteries. MacKinnon's notion of how sex can be used seems to rest on the unspoken assumption that sexuality "is" a devil, a kind of irresistible temptation, an infinitely manipulable weakness — like hunger in time of famine, which can be exploited to get people to do anything one wants, rather than like appetite, which is cultivated and formed by fantasy.

This assessment of sexuality actually slams the door on the provocative question as to how sex can be violence and violence can be sex. What exactly allows sexuality to carry or transmit relations of power, violence, and destruction? What is this "thing" called sex? The collaboration between sexuality and power might somehow be related to the fact that a violation that would be abominable in reality can be pleasurable in fantasy. The disjunction between fantasy and reality must be taken seriously if we are to begin to understand the complexity of sexuality and its inveterate association with violence and revulsion.

The violent character that sexuality assumes in fantasy is not simply the unconscious content coming to light, the opening of Pandora's box, as early psychoanalytic discussions seemed to imply. In what might be seen as the flip side of Dworkin's literal-mindedness, psychoanalysts formerly took literally the idea that the lifting of repression revealed an unconscious wish —for instance, that women's unconscious wish to be ravaged constituted the trauma of rape. This supposition reflected a simple inversion of the notion that people want what they consciously express, that reality lies on the surface of consciousness. It collapsed the distinction between the symbolic meaning expressed by such a wish and its literal enactment, between the symbolic and the concrete, between experiences that can be symbolized and those too painful and traumatic to be symbolically processed. Emphasizing this distinction, Simone de Beauvoir (1949) pointed out that even if the adolescent girl enjoys the fantasy of being raped, the reality of rape would be traumatic, horrible. The presence of an other who is outside one's control and can exert power on one's body is an entirely different experience from any fantasy form of the wish, however frightening. Despite the efforts of feminists to bring the traumatic meaning of real events to the foreground (see Herman 1992; Davies and Frawley 1993), psychoanalysis took an inordinate amount of time to begin to grasp the difference between trauma and fantasy. On the other hand, fantasy plays a role in representing and concealing real horror that a simple insistence on reality misses.

As most psychoanalysts have finally admitted, reported experiences of incestuous abuse often are not imagined but represent real trauma; the effects of real events are usually quite different from those of imagined interactions, even though the latter may constitute efforts to represent less explicit actions. The manifold consequences of abuse, especially dissociative states, and the complexity that these consequences generate in the analytic process, especially in the transference-countertransference (Davies and Frawley 1993), are finally receiving serious attention. In light of such efforts, it becomes apparent that what is presumably real is often the most difficult thing for the mind to take in and process symbolically — it is "hard to believe." The acknowledgment of reality does not mean that fantasy is now entirely reducible to reality, or even that fantasy does not play a role in the individual's representation of traumatic events, although often the ability to make good use of fantasy is impaired. It means that the "truth" resides not merely in the wish but also in the place of the wish in relation to real events and fantasized objects; that the subject takes a different position toward the one than toward the other; and that the inability to own reality (denial) is as serious a problem as the inability to own fantasy (repression).

The ability to distinguish fantasy from real events and to use symbolic representation to signify something other than its concrete referent cuts both ways. The antipornography movement operates with the same concreteness of thought, in reverse, as did the old psychoanalysts. By equating representations of fantasy with reality, the movement suggests that images of violation are as traumatic as the reality of violent events — when, in fact, those images may be used to represent something different or farther flung. The same false oppositions frame polarized debates in other sexual arenas, so that political discussions of sexual harassment, date-rape, and recovered memory often manufacture impossible choices between paranoia and denial of real abuse.

It is necessary, therefore, to protect the distinction between the symbolic and the concrete on two fronts — to sustain simultaneously the respect for unconscious fantasy life and for outer reality, a tension that threatens to break down both in the psychoanalytic movement and in intellectual life as a whole. This tension corresponds to the two main difficulties in dealing with destructiveness: recognizing real danger "out there" and accepting the presence of internal destructiveness.

To begin with, then, pornographic representations express not the concrete content of desire but rather a relation between sexual excitement and the realm of fantasy. The character of pornographic representation, especially its sadistic content, charges us to formulate the distinction between reality and fantasy — between being affected by an outside other and being inside the enclosure of one's own fantasy, between the concrete and the symbolic. The conflicting reactions that pornographic representations generate — arousal and resentment — point to this distinction. They also point beyond the individual to the collective or cultural dimension of such representation as a "shared imaginary" of sexuality. Thus pornography itself, as a kind of social institution or agency, has a liminal status. It contains a direct appeal to a private world of fantasy, and yet it is a source of outside stimulation, which can be felt to manipulate or do violence to the conscious self by stimulating against one's will, by evoking the unconscious imagery and identifications one has to share with others. Pornography can therefore be felt as a confrontation with some dangerous and exciting otherness, fictive or real, which has the power to create internal excitement, pleasurable and/or repellent. It may be that this otherness is all the more repellent at times because it corresponds to an other that lives within us, making us, as Kristeva (1991) put it, "strangers to ourselves."

Understanding this confrontation depends, I have been suggesting, not only on how we think about sexuality but also on how we think about the relations between fantasy and reality, inside and outside, self and other. The decisive issue may not be the content of sadism — for we assume that sadistic elements are present in all sexual life — but rather the counterpoint between fantasy and recognition of otherness, especially the other's subjectivity.

My point of departure is Bataille's (1962) provocative question: How is eroticism related to death? Why do images of death and violence inspire sexual excitement? This question in turn will lead us to some speculation about the transformation of mental material into bodily, sexual excitement, about what it means that fantasies "go into the body." Bataille's reflections on eroticism are in much the same vein as Freud's portrayal of the struggle between life and death. At the beginning of *Death and Sensuality* Bataille quotes Sade: "There is no better way to know death than to link it with some licentious image." Freud's (1931) opinion is quite close to this: the death instinct "escapes detection unless its presence is betrayed by its being alloyed with Eros."

In Bataille's thinking, death is a point of reference for the loss of differentiation between self and other: "Eroticism opens the way to death. Death opens the way to the denial of our individual lives. Without doing violence to our inner selves, are we able to bear a negation that carries us to the farthest bounds of possibility?" (p. 24). By "death" Bataille means not literal death but "the fusion of separate objects" that ends their separate identities, a dissolution of the self. Bataille's picture is paradoxical: individual islands separated by a sea of death — representing the ultimate oneness — which the isolates must cross to meet one another. It is this crossing that creates sexual excitement: "But I cannot refer to this gulf which separates us without feeling that this is not the whole truth of the matter. It is a deep gulf, and I do not see how it can be done away with. Nonetheless, we can experience its dizziness *together*. It can hypnotize us. This gulf is death in one sense, and death is vertiginous, death is hypnotizing" (pp. 12–13).

When we experience together the gulf that separates us, we recognize our mutual condition. It is evident that the perspective from which Bataille develops his analysis of the relationship between eroticism and death includes the relationship between self and other. This perspective — implied by the question of whether we experience death together — is the intersubjective dimension. This dimension may turn out to be as important for understanding erotic life as is the fantasmic labyrinth of the unconscious that intrapsychic theory opens up to us.

The recognition by separate beings of commonality is the central phenomenon referred to in the intersubjective dimension. In my view that term best describes the level of conceptualizing interaction that is backgrounded by intrapsychic theory, the concern not with the vicissitudes of instincts or the content of unconscious fantasy but with the status of recognition between subjects. Because this level has often been implicit in intrapsychic theory, my intent is not to replace intrapsychic theory with an intersubjective theory but rather to make that level explicit. As I discussed in Chapter 1, the two theoretical perspectives are complementary though not always congruent; they can be used in tandem to view the same experience. In regard to sexuality and fantasy, the issues Freud grasped in the metaphors of instinct theory have their counterpart in intersubjective theory. If we cannot always interpret simultaneously in both dimensions, we can translate between them. Specifically, the conflict between Eros and Thanatos — Freud's (1931) own metaphor here is the Devil, the principle of destructiveness — can be translated into the terms of the conflict between recognition and destruction of the other. But this translation will not afford a one-to-one relation between the terms.

As a psychological category, intersubjectivity refers to the capacity of the mind to directly register the responses of the other. It is affected by whether the other recognizes what we have done and is likewise charged with recognizing the other's acts. Above all intersubjectivity refers to our capacity to recognize the other as an independent subject. In the mutual exchange (or denial) of recognition, each self is transformed; this transformation is a condition of each subject's expression (or denial) of her or his own capacities. Whatever breakdowns in recognition occur, as they inevitably do, the primary intersubjective condition of erotic life is that of "experiencing the dizziness *together.*"

Is this reference to shared experience simply a statement of the obvious? Does it denature Bataille's radical embrace of transgression to note that psychoanalytic and philosophical writers from widely different perspectives might join in this sentiment? The core experience of intersubjectivity, as Daniel Stern (1985) has analyzed it in his work on the development of infant consciousness, is that separate minds can share common states, feelings, or experiences. In Winnicott's (1969b) thinking, which approaches the problem of recognition from a very different vantage point, the intersubjective moment is placed later, after an early state of undifferentiation, as a breaking out of omnipotence. In that moment we are able to differentiate between the subjectively conceived object and the objective object, which is an entity in its own right. Thus the distinction is not merely between the infant hallucinating the breast and the arrival of the real, as in Freud's (1915a) concept of the reality principle; it is between perceiving the real breast as if it were simply an extension of one's wish and perceiving it as an outside entity that provides not-me substance (Winnicott 1969b; see Eigen 1981). Intersubjectively speaking, the same breast, or the same sexual fantasy, can thus be experienced in two different positions.

Recognition means that the other is mentally placed in the position of a different, outside entity but shares a similar feeling or state of mind. Separate minds and bodies can attune. In erotic union this attunement can be so intense that the separation between self and other feels momentarily suspended: self and other are fused. The sense of losing the self in the other and that of really being known for oneself can be reconciled. This sense of simultaneously losing the self and retaining wholeness is often called *oneness* and is often described as the ultimate point of erotic union. The desire for erotic union with another person who is endowed with the capacity to transform the self can be seen as the most intense version of the desire for recognition. When both individuals experience themselves as being transformed by the other, or by what they create in conjunction with the other, a choreography emerges that is not reducible to the idea of reacting to the outside. The experience is one not only of sensual pleasure, which can be felt in a state of aloneness or indifference to the other's existence, but of co-creation and mutual recognition. In erotic union the point is to contact and be contacted by the other — *apprehended as such*.

The risk of such declarative statements about the erotic is that one seems to set up an ideal or essence against which everything else is measured as alienated or epiphenomenal. So I hasten to add that erotic recognition does not ever occur in some independent realm, purified of the unconscious fantasy stuff that dreams are made of. Recognition is the act of the same subject whose mental life is full of such stuff. The significance of recognition or its absence can be thought of as something like that of a metacomment: a statement about the position of the erotic partners in assuming the togetherness of their fantasies. Is a common fantasy and its accompanying mood—for example, "No matter how wild you become, I will always feel safe with you; no matter how insatiable I feel, you will always be able to satisfy me, and this is what makes it so wonderful to be with you"—shared by both partners (see Hollibaugh and Moraga 1983)? Does the disruption of this fantasy feel intolerable, or the perpetuation of it coercive? Does fantasy remain a fluid medium, to be reinvented and transformed, or is it hardened into objective forms of interaction that cease to convey any sense of reaching or being transformed by the other? The presence or absence of power fantasies is not the issue; it is their intersubjective context that is decisive.

The relevance of this intersubjective dimension becomes evident as we examine the fate of Bataille's flirtation with death through transgression. Significantly, Bataille draws back from the joint contemplation of the abyss in his text and goes on to present instead the familiar form of dissolution, the dual unity of violator and violated—male and female, of course. In my analysis of erotic domination as exemplified by *Story of O* (Benjamin 1988), I argued that this breakdown into complementarity of doer and done to—so taken for granted by Bataille—reflects the inability to sustain the necessary contradiction of differentiation, in which we both recognize the other and continue to assert the self. In this breakdown these two elements of differentiation are split: one self asserts power, the other recognizes that power through submission. The two moments are represented as opposite and distinct tendencies, so that they are available to the subject only as alternatives: each can play only one side at a time, projecting the opposite side onto the other (and, of course, these alternatives are organized by gender, in the form of the oedipal complementarity). In the split unity, each partner represents the other's opposite rather than struggling fully with the other for recognition.

It is the rigidity of this complementarity that ultimately leads to narrative exhaustion, the moribund outcome of objectification. The shared confrontation with de-differentiation — that is, the dizzying loss of self in erotic experience — is what counteracts the element of one person's reducing the other to his (undifferentiated) thing. As the splitting of positions into violator and violated gradually vitiates the shared sensibility, vertigo is replaced by control. The sexual tension diminishes as the master overpowers the other's subjectivity.[1] Loss of tension is the common dynamic of erotic domination and objectification. Thus the split unity of violator and violated eventually reproduces the same deadness and lack of sexual tension that the vertiginous confrontation with death was meant to overcome. The sea of death can be crossed only by reaching the other — as a being outside omnipotent control.

In the analysis of sexual transgression from the intrapsychic viewpoint, the effort to reduce the other also appears as a reaction to the threat of engulfment and the concern with differentiation. The work of the psychoanalyst Janine Chasseguet-Smirgel has focused on the intrapsychic meanings of perversion and explored the content of sadistic fantasies. Chasseguet-Smirgel (1984) has interpreted Sade's fantasies as anal sadism:

---

1. As Bataille (1976) recognized, "the slave by accepting defeat . . . has lost the quality without which he is unable to *recognize* the conqueror so as to satisfy him. The slave is unable to give the master the *satisfaction* without which the master can no longer rest" (p. 12).

she proposes that Sade's core fantasy is the reduction of the maternal body to shit, the reduction of all nature through the digestive tract into an undifferentiated mass. The key argument here is that sadism reflects an anal striving toward de-differentiation, a breaking of the paternal-genital law of separation. This view of de-differentiation builds on Freud's notion of aggression as the turning outward of the death instinct, which strives to reduce everything to its original, undifferentiated state.

What is the relationship between the intrapsychic and the intersubjective understandings of sadism? As I have said, the two positions are not necessarily in conflict or mutually exclusive. The intrapsychic formulation insists on the visceral body of fantasy, specifically, on the importance of anality. But what does anality, with its well-known association with sadism, actually mean? In fact, as I shall suggest, the turning of passive into active, inner into outer, must play a vital role in this association. Chasseguet-Smirgel's interpretation of sadism as the de-differentiation of the object by alimentary reduction does not fully elaborate the function of anal sadism for the self in relation to other. Her analysis emphasizes only one side of the sadistic act. The act aims not only at de-differentiating the other, as she points out, but also at differentiating the self: the self imagines that in reducing the other it is establishing its own identity. Because it imagines that in digesting the other it is nourishing its own identity, its effort to gain control over the other actually represents an effort to separate, to achieve its own autonomy. The paradigmatic other who is being reduced is the mother, from whom the sadist feels unable to separate.

As Stoller (1975) argued, in his discussion of perversion, sadism tries to both "do and undo differentiation." It not only breaks the paternal law of separation but desperately tries at the same time to reinforce it (and this, incidentally, may cast some doubt upon the paternal law itself). The sadistic erotic fantasies, which may then attract adult men to pornographic sadism, usually represent a retaliatory reversal of the omnipotent control suffered at the mother's hands. The impotent rage that the child has split off, unable to express or encompass, reappears in the sexualized fantasy — fueled not by eros but by aggression. (For that matter, women may identify with these fantasies for similar reasons; and men as well as women may play the part of the mother who suffers the child's attack.) The child's wishes for differentiation are transformed but recognizable in the sadistic fantasy: the wish to finally reach the mother as well as to punish her, to separate from her as well as to control her, to be recognized by her as well as to obliterate her.

Whereas the intersubjective understanding of transgression emphasizes the effort to differentiate self and other and simultaneously to absorb the other, the intrapsychic view emphasizes the vicissitudes of aggression and sexuality. In the intrapsychic view, sadism is a reaction to a primary condition of the instinct, a way of discharging the impulse toward reduction and de-differentiation (the death instinct); in the intersubjective view the primary condition is the predicament of simultaneously recognizing self and other (object), and sadism is a reaction to difficulties that may result from the vicissitudes of that predicament. Is there a place where these two vectors of understanding can intersect, creating a multidimensional picture?

The paradoxical doing and undoing of differentiation can be seen as a reaction to the primary condition of intersubjectivity, the predicament of needing an other who is outside our control — to the imaginary threat of assimilating or being assimilated by the other. We must consider the ways in which different perspectives define this need for the other and the threat it poses.

The metaphor of the death instinct, recast in light of self-other differentiation, helps to link the idea of loss of tension to the trajectories of sexuality and aggression. The advantage of Freud's theory of the death instinct is that these links are clearly established, even though in the final analysis "instinct" may best be understood not literally, biologically, but rather as a metaphor for somatic and affective states. Freud's discussions of sadism and the death instinct were an attempt to understand the repetition compulsion — the endlessly frustrating replay of destructiveness. He concluded, with some reluctance (1920), that an explanation of the repetition compulsion required postulation of a death drive that impels us toward complete absence of tension. Projecting the death drive outward in the form of aggression or mastery was the only protection against succumbing to it. As I have said elsewhere (Benjamin 1988), this understanding of aggression can be seen as Freud's effort to explain domination, and in this sense as a parallel story to the master-slave paradox. The absence of intersubjective tension or dissolution of otherness that accompanies domination corresponds, of course, to Freud's repetition compulsion. Domination of the other is the result of the conversion of the death drive into mastery or aggression.

Freud (1931) brings together the idea of destructiveness, the primary drive toward utter nothingness, and the incarnation of evil. He points out in a footnote to *Civilization and Its Discontents*, "In Goethe's Mephistopheles we have a quite exceptionally convincing identification of the principle of evil with the destructive instinct." He quotes the devil: "Everything that comes to be, deserves to be destroyed (Denn alles, was entsteht, Ist wert, dass es zu Grund geht). . . . Destruction, aught with Evil blent, That is my proper element (So ist dann alles, was Ihr Sunde nennt, Zerstörung, kurz das Böse nennt, Mein eigentliches Element)." And further, he tells us, "The Devil himself names as his adversary, not what is holy and good, but Nature's power to create, to multiply life — that is Eros" (pp. 120–121).[2] Freud misses the implication of this association to Nature: that the power to create life, Eros, might be identified as a maternal principle, envied and attacked by those who do not possess it. He does announce that civilization presents "the struggle between Eros and Death, between the instinct of life and the instinct of destruction" (p. 122).

Aggression has to contend with its "immortal adversary," Eros, which may fuse with and defuse it. Eros in general, and sexuality in particular, neutralize aggression. Freud writes that the life and death instincts almost never appear in isolation, but "are alloyed with each other . . . and so become unrecognizable. In sadism . . . we should have before us a particularly strong alloy of this kind between trends of love and the destructive instinct; while its counterpart, masochism, would be a union between destructiveness directed inwards and sexuality" (p. 119).

The best place to observe and analyze destructiveness is in erotic life, perhaps the only place to grasp the otherwise elusive death instinct:

> It is in sadism, where the death instinct twists the erotic aim in its own sense, and yet at the same time fully satisfies the erotic urge, that we succeed in obtaining the clearest insight into its nature, and its relation to Eros. But even where it emerges without any sexual purpose, in the blindest fury of destructiveness, we cannot fail to recognize that the satisfaction of the instinct is accompanied by an extraordinarily high degree of narcissistic enjoyment, owing to its presenting the ego with a fulfillment of the latter's old wishes for omnipotence (p. 121).

2. Freud further complicates the picture by suggesting that splitting is at work. He adds that in view of his own unwillingness to admit the necessity of destructiveness, he understands that the Devil is "the best way out as an excuse for God . . . playing the same part as an agent of economic discharge as the Jew does in the world of the Aryan ideal."

Immediately before this statement Freud interjects a short explanation of how he moved from the instinctual dualism of ego instinct versus object instincts (libido) to the dualism of death instinct versus libido. So it is a fair reading that death (aggression) now holds the place of narcissism (omnipotence) in the theory, a transposition that has become increasingly significant to our current understanding of narcissism. By the end of this discussion, it appears that destruction "satisfies" the ego instinct, the narcissistic wish for omnipotence. What are we entitled to make of this imbrication of the destructive instinct and narcissism? Doesn't it raise the possibility that destructiveness is routed directly through the ego's wish for omnipotence —an idea that places aggression only a split hair away from insistence on absolute selfhood? Omnipotence—that is, the loss/obliteration of the outside other—might be seen as the intersubjective correlate of what Freud calls the death instinct.

Let us say, then, that mental omnipotence is the fantasy counterpart to death—metaphorically, it is the loss of tension between inside and outside, the absolute return of the self to itself. Omnipotence (whether it refers to the pole of merging or the pole of withdrawal, to union with or aggression against the other, to oneness or all-aloneness) means the complete assimilation of the other into the self. It signifies a flat line on the graph, the complete reduction of tension between self and other in mental representation. Mastery, as Freud thinks about it, is both an expression of death/omnipotence and an effort to escape it: to create tension, to break up this assimilation of or by the other, which will allow nothing to exist outside. Yet in the equation death = aggression, the death instinct is final, it has the last word, at least as long as the monadic self is encapsulated in a closed system, the omnipotent mind, and cannot reach something outside. The destructive energy is always "conserved" within the system, always comes back to haunt the self.

Perhaps we must return to this feature of the instinct, its conservatism, its conservation within the encapsulated self. If we postulate that the self's relation to its own tension is dependent upon its tension with the other, we are calling into question the inevitability of the self's encapsulation, and hence the conservation of destructive energy that Freud proposes. Freud's notion of instinct, specifically of the conversion of the death instinct into aggression, and from aggression into outward mastery, includes the equally important idea of expression or discharge. The object or outside must, in fact, receive the energy that the subject is directing toward it. It is this exchange between inside and outside, self and other, that, as Brennan (1992) emphasizes, constitutes the intersubjective element in Freud's theory. The other must receive or contain what the subject puts out. Her reading of Freud's theory makes room within it for the possibility of an intersubjective "way out" of omnipotence and the consequent conservation of the death instinct.

Perhaps, then, rather than to express death as simply a metaphor for loss of self-other tension, we ought to consider the way that tension moves from inside to outside. To translate the notion of a drive toward death (zero tension) into omnipotence (loss of tension between self and other) does not fully confront the question of how the two terms, inside and outside, are actually connected. Eigen (1993), embracing both intrapsychic and intersubjective theory, offers some insight into this matter with an interpretation of sadism related to the primal experience of "stimulus rape." The early flooding of sensations that the infant must passively experience can be conceptualized as a primary masochism, the source of "the death wish" (a notion Freud considered in *Beyond the Pleasure Principle*). This primary need to reduce tension may be seen as the origin of the inversion that Freud described, whereby "the death wish" is turned outward as aggression. Aggression and its derivative, mastery, represent the effort to turn outward the invading stimuli, the unbearable tension. In the face of an original intolerable helplessness, the ego defends itself through the well-known switch from passive to active (Christiansen 1993).

But something is missing from our formulation. Without the outside other, there is no one, no thing, to help the originally helpless subject to absorb, process, and tolerate states of internal tension. Freud's energic, economic view can be understood as a metaphor for experiences of the monadic self—that is, for internal regulation of tension. This formulation of the death instinct as the drive to reduce tension should perhaps be linked to the intersubjective need for a sustaining tension between self and other that makes internal tension bearable. Here is the first other as "transformational object" (Bollas 1987) or regulator of states (Beebe and Lachmann 1994).

Only retroactively—at what point of differentiation we are not sure—does a person become able to represent the other as outside and the other's help in relieving tension as not-self. And, to further obscure the matter, by the time a child is able to differentiate, she or he has learned to regulate a good deal of her or his own tension. Still, this representation of distinct self and other does exist. So we must ask: Under what conditions does a process between subjects appear as part of the mental life of the single subject, as purely internal, as the inner compulsion that the subject wants to fulfill or escape? In intersubjective terms, the self that has to escape an overwhelming tension caused by stimulus outside its control is never an isolated self: if no other is there to help contain that tension, it is still registered (although perhaps not able to be represented) as the absent other, who could have or should have been there (Green 1986). If absence becomes traumatic, the self cannot represent it, yet is still haunted by the one who wasn't there. For the isolated self, too overwhelmed and alone to represent the other, what appears is not the other's absence but rather death, or the wish for death. Such traumatic, unrepresented loss can become the basis for sexual fantasies of submission and domination, as Khan (1979) showed.

More generally, to be able to represent the absence of the other means to experience the absence of someone felt to exist outside mental omnipotence, someone who can contain the tension that we cannot bear alone, who can receive what it is necessary to give. As Winnicott (1969b) emphasized, the baby who has made the transition into "using the object" is able to represent the other as an outside being who relieves tension; the baby experiences an "outside breast" rather than an extension of self. The usable object emerges only through surviving destruction: the effort to break out of omnipotence by placing the other outside one's fantasy, to apprehend her or him as external reality. In his view the subject begins in the state of omnipotence, and yet the other (mother) is always already there, giving omnipotence the lie, receiving, containing, and regulating excitement that would otherwise be unbearable.[3] The question is how this function of the other can begin to be felt as outside rather than as an extension of self. The answer is that the assertion of omnipotence in the form of aggression or negation of

3. As I have already indicated, there are certain problems with the assumption that the child begins in the state of omnipotence. I am not sure that understanding omnipotence as a sequential category — a starting point — is necessary to Winnicott's theory, and it may lead to certain misunderstandings. The contradiction between the felt connection to the other and the "omnipotence of thoughts," the child's view that reality is inside her or his control, may mean that omnipotence and outsideness have to be constituted simultaneously. Both would then begin when the child starts to realize meaningfully that reality is in fact outside control. Before that, the child is relating sometimes to the outside other, sometimes to fantasy, without differentiating but also without a notion of control. It may be that Winnicott's category of creative illusion is more useful for the state of undifferentiation, that of omnipotence for the state when the contradiction becomes apparent and the other's response or susceptibility to control becomes represented.

the other collides with the barrier of the (m)other's continuing existence. Whereas the (m)other's survival permits the shattering of mental omnipotence, her failure to survive leaves the subject with unprocessed, indigestible rage that cannot be further broken down and metabolized. This overwhelming, unmanageable internal tension, which is not contained by the other's holding or communication, remains as aggression. Alongside it is the unrepresentable absence of the other who has not survived. These experiences of loss and aggression can be split off and become the basis for the perverse and sadistic elements of sexual fantasy that we associate with pornography and compulsive sexual activity.

If no outside is recognized, there is no relational space in which to put one's own excitement and aggression, no one else to recognize and process it. This insight was decisively formulated and elaborated by Bion (1962a, b) in his discussions of the container mother and the need for mental digestion; thus it is central to post-Kleinian thought. As Winnicott succinctly put it in relation to the analyst, if the other is not outside and is only "a subjective phenomenon, what about waste disposal?" (p. 107). Likewise, unless mother's external subjectivity is registered, there is no reassurance against fantasies (her own or the child's) of her omnipotence, her seduction, or her control: the fantasies of the mother's body as overwhelming or invasive are not countered by an experience of mutual recognition.[4] There is no experience that can contribute to a symbolic representation of the mother's body as both permeable to one's own feel-

---

4. Again, I want to stress that mutual recognition does not imply perfect knowledge or attunement; nor, as Aron has emphasized, does it require complete symmetry. Nonetheless, the reciprocity of giving and taking, acting and having an impact, communicating and negotiating difference creates space. This space is not only permeable, it also works as a boundary against invasion, a condition of freedom that makes it possible to give and receive something uncoerced (Zoltan Szankay, personal communication; see also Szankay, 1994).

ings and unattacking. When we refer to recognition of the mother as an independent subject we are including this notion of a mother who is both (partially, imperfectly) knowable and knowing, who can be affected without being annihilated, who can encompass what is inside us without imposing terrifying fantasies from within her. She is neither overwhelmingly weak/needy nor invincible/perfect — as in the fantasies of the mother as a controlling, coercive figure that invariably underlie sadistic fantasy.

In a sense, sadistic fantasies are the quintessential expression of inability to recognize the mother as the imperfect but external subject, the inability to tolerate outsideness or otherness that arises from failed destruction. Sadistic fantasies reflect the absence of an external object that sets a limit to the subject's mind, that survives. As Eigen (1993) has analyzed it, Sade's fantasies are a protest against any outside reality, any limitation set by nature: Sade deliberately excludes the vagina and makes "*woman's* asshole the primary sexual object . . . emphasizing the import of his *choice*" (p. 100; emphasis Eigen's). Insisting on his absolute freedom to define sexuality, Sade rejects the bodily givens of homosexuality (man's mouth and anus) as well as heterosexuality, "carrying his protest to infinity." In other words, absolutely everything is his to decide; his is a refusal not merely of differentiation but of the outside world, a "transcendental reversal" (p. 101).

As I have discussed in relation to Winnicott's theory (see Chapters 1 and 3; Benjamin 1988), the freedom to fantasize may contribute positively to the metabolizing of aggression; the exercise of that freedom may help to dissipate the sense of unreality that disappointment and rage have engendered. The inner tension of aggression may be modified through a shift in the outer relationship back to mutual understanding, which includes communication of fantasy contents. Rather than bouncing back in retaliation (as in the child's rejoinder to name-calling, "I'm rubber, you're glue; everything you say bounces off me and sticks to you"), the other's persistence in receiving communication gives meaning to the expressive act and so transforms the self's inner state. The transformation is in the direction that permits the self once again to tolerate the outside, the different. The shift back to mutual understanding, or out of the fantasy of destruction into the reality of survival, reestablishes the tension between two individuals even as it dissipates the tension of aggression within the individual. But when this shift back to intersubjective reality fails, internalization remains the only way to deal with aggression; the turning inward of aggression forms the basis of the fantasy of doer and done to, an inner world of persecutors and victims.

The apparent busyness of this inner world does not alter the essential emptiness that is felt when the self assimilates to other or other is assimilated to the self. Deadness and repetition reflect the inability to contact anything outside. In this case internal fantasy replaces rather than complements interaction or exchange with the outside.

This turning inward of aggression when the other fails to survive may be a key to understanding certain forms of sexual fantasy. In my analysis of erotic domination (1980) I suggest a parallel between Winnicott's thinking about the destruction of the object and Freud's (1915a) discussion of sadomasochism in "Instincts and Their Vicissitudes." In Freud's thinking at that time (the period in which he defined the instincts as self-preservation and libido, before the formulation of the death instinct), the infant's initial posture is that of a primary sadism.[5] This

---

5. Again, though, I find Eigen's argument convincing that beneath this primary sadism we can postulate an even more primary experience of "stimulus rape," producing the inner tension that leads to the initial aggression. However, in this logic aggression is absolutely ineluctable, since there is always more tension than can be

sadism is indifferent to the outcome, to whether or not the other is being hurt. Perhaps it is simply a discharge of aggression, before consequences are perceived. The intervening step that leads to the formation of true sadism is that the child internalizes and turns this sadism against him- or herself, in the form of a primary masochism. Finally, once the identification with suffering is in place, the infliction of pain on the other — sadism proper — emerges. In other words, it is only the step of internalization that converts the primary destructive impulse into a wish to harm.

Laplanche (1976) elaborates this movement from primary sadism to masochism to sadism proper in a suggestive way. He proposes that we call the first step aggression rather than sadism, for initially it is not alloyed with sexuality at all. It becomes alloyed with sexuality only in the second step, at the point where it is internalized as masochism. Thus, only with the second step — masochism — do we have the first sexual position. This turning around on the subject, the move toward reflexivity, is actually what creates sexuality (pp. 92–102). Independently of whether the fantasy itself is of being active or passive, it is central to both sadism and masochism. In both the dominant and the submissive role, the action is internalized and enters the self as fantasy. The process of turning around occurs through the transmutation of aggression into "the sexual" — what Laplanche calls fantasmatization — regardless of the fantasy content. In this reflexive process, Laplanche states, "the fantasy, the unconscious, and sexuality" emerge "in a single movement." This sexuality, he argues, is actually a kind of "frenetic anti-life," opposed to Eros (pp. 123–126).

---

somatically and mentally processed, except in death. In keeping with Freud's later argument in *Beyond the Pleasure Principle*, escaping tension is the logic behind the death wish, turning the tension outward in aggression the preferred means of escape.

Although I may be taking liberties with Laplanche's intentions, I believe that in his theory of the creation of sexuality as a process of fantasmatization he is describing something similar to Winnicott's theory of destruction and survival. Of course, he is working with the language of instinctual tension as the property of the monad, and so we are once again required to translate. But his novel reading of the meaning of sadism suggests an important point of intersection with the idea of the destruction of the object, one that leads to a new understanding of sexuality. We might refer to what Laplanche calls sexuality as "the sexual"—a sexuality that is not Eros but seems closer to what Bataille usually means by eroticism.[6] We might suppose that fantasmatization means a process of symbolically re-turning aggression into one's body, where it is converted into a source of pleasure—a reprocessing of bodily tension in the imaginary body. This conversion of aggression is the essential mechanism for the creation of the realm of sexual fantasy. This realm of fantasy then relates to the "subjectively conceived object," as opposed to the independent object who has survived destruction and can be loved—even if both objects are the same person.

Eros, as Laplanche, following Freud, implies, is about something other than the sexual; it is about life as opposed to death, about contacting the other. Again, this does not mean that Eros designates some purified relationship to the other that is free of aggression or hate. Quite the contrary, Eros, like "the sexual," has its own way of taking up aggression and sexuality—of balancing recognition and destruction. But the erotic moment is that in which the other survives destruction, is not wholly assimilable to one's mental product. It is about the en-

6. For Bataille (1962), the juxtaposition is between sexuality as something purely animal and eroticism as that which involves our encounter with death. See *Les Larmes d'Eros*.

counter of two subjects that moves through omnipotence to re-create tension, that includes mutual recognition or the sharing of mental states. But such definitions do not mean that "the sexual" and the erotic can be teased apart, for they generally occur simultaneously.

I would like to consider the idea that the sadomasochistic themes so common in fantasy and in cultural representations of gender, especially pornography, are the logical culmination of the turning inward of action and the creation of fantasmic sexuality, "the sexual." Ultimately, they are a means of dealing with encapsulation in omnipotence in the absence of intersubjective containment of: aggression, loss, or trauma leading to unrepresentable psychic pain. This absence has resulted in a disproportionate disappearance of the outside other. In its place appears the objectified "subjectively conceived" object, a fantasmic being that does not solve the problem of "waste disposal." We might say, then, that the pornographic use of sadomasochistic fantasy reflects an attempt to turn outward a sexuality that is already turned in on itself. Like the third step in Freud's discussion of sadomasochism, it follows upon a turning inward. It is a reaction to the unpleasant inner tension associated with the absence of outer tension — a state we call boredom — or to the unmanageable surfeit of tension we call rage, which perhaps marks the place of the unrepresentable pain and loss that must be enacted through the imagery of bodily pain. In particular, directing aggression toward and inflicting pain on the female body serves a double purpose: substituting for the intersubjective container of communication and representation, and revenge against the mother for failing to respond.

Sexual boredom is frequently the reason given for an interest in pornography. But the dilemma then becomes how to turn back outward when there is no outside, when both subject and object exist only within the capsule of omnipotence, of fantasy. This is where transgression comes in, the attempt to create a substitute form of outsideness by exposing the inner, private, autoerotic components to a fantasied public, to an observer that is neither subject nor object of the fantasy. The spectator creates the sense of outsideness, the consumer is the outside other to his own fantasy, which is enacted on the screen or the page before him.

This transgressive breakthrough between inside and outside can become simply another loop in the circuit of doomed efforts to reach some live connection, some externality. The point of such contact is, of course, discharge — discharge of aggression, evacuation of toxic elements, and embodiment of the pain or degradation that cannot be encompassed by the self. Discharge into an outside that does not exist in mental representation is impossible; some tension with the outside is required to produce physical discharge. Lacking the opportunity to rid the self of aggression, the subject transmutes it into sexual discharge; autoeroticism affords a substitute behavior that seemingly does not require an outside other. Whereas in infancy the regulation of internal tension states has to occur through the direct transformational action of self or other, the pornographic subject can partially use the symbolic level for transformation and can identify with representations of bodily activity. In another sense, however, his or her use of images bears comparison with infantile self-regulation through autoerotic self-stimulation. The use of symbolism in pornography is incomplete; it does not serve to release tension without physical stimulation and discharge (as, for instance, the close of a narrative may produce emotional discharge, catharsis, through identification). Indeed, the purpose of pornography is to use but attenuate symbolic expression, to evoke excitement that can be released through physical self-stimulation. What this suggests is a kind of interruption in the symbolic processing — again, not primarily of sexuality but of aggression. We may ask whether, as Laplanche implies, this interruption is a derivative of joining excitement to the fantasmatic (see Stoller 1975).

Let us consider the matter of symbolization for a moment. Difficulties in symbolization (see Freedman 1980) refer us to the thing that is missed when two subjects are not able to realize or negotiate difference: along with the representation of an other, the potential space of symbolization (Green 1986; Ogden 1986) also dissolves. If the intersubjective space of symbolic play transforms omnipotence, allowing the subject to return to a world of mutual understanding, it also preserves-by-transforming omnipotence fantasies by transposing them into another form through sublimation. When the other survives confrontations over assertion and difference, when aggression is "caught" by the other, then there is a space of symbolic communication between subjects in which disappointment or excitement can be contained. With the emergence of this space between the person and the action, between action and reaction, it becomes possible to symbolize feeling in fantasy and words.

To complete the move from physical discharge (e.g., of aggression) to symbolic elaboration presumes the intersubjective space of communication. The space between self and other also makes possible a space between symbol and object (Ogden 1986). The object is not equated with symbolic properties attributed to it, as in "She is that thing I fear," but rather is seen as distinct from those properties (see Chapter 3). The ability to recognize the symbolic properties of the object as one's own attributions reflects the differentiation between self and other. Thus the development of the self-other relationship allows the development of symbolic capacities out of the symbolic equation (Segal 1957) into true symbolization, in which fantasy and reality are no longer interchangeable (Freedman 1980).

"Things" are not what they are, or even what they are felt to be; they are not made equivalent by the verb "to be," as in the statement "Violence *is* sex when it is practiced as sex."

In the absence of intersubjective space, symbolic capacities collapse: actions become things, and images of actions become things. If the consumer of pornography takes the image as an occasion for physical discharge, so the opponents of pornography likewise collapse representation and action. Antipornographers say, in effect, "These images *make* me feel bad," rather than "I feel bad when I see this because I identify with the image of myself as a degraded object." Or even, "Because of my identification, because I am moved by such things and they do not leave me cold, I should at least be free to avoid having to see them on public display." Instead, the argument has been posed in terms of "real" effects. The antipornography campaign has said, "I cannot take this to be symbolic; it is the same to me as if the act were actually being performed upon me." Indeed, for those people who have suffered abusive and traumatizing violence, it is not surprising that the space of symbolization has been destroyed as well, that the image conveys the threat of actuality, as Dworkin's autobiographical confession has made clear. Both pornography and antipornographers operate on the basis of the symbolic equation, in which what is represented in the image is not symbolic but real: the controversy is only about whether the "thing" is sex or violence. The symbol is the thing symbolized; the representation itself *is* violence. The self feels coerced by the thing, deprived of subjectivity by the objectifying image. As a result of the foreclosure of the symbolic space, representations of violence undertaken with the artistic intent of evoking meaningful reflection cannot be discriminated from violence meant to excite coercively.

But if the same underlying structure — the symbolic equation — underlies both real acts of symbolic violence and the pornographic representation, this does not make action and representation exactly the same (Stoller 1985). Violence is violence when it is practiced as violence, to paraphrase MacKinnon. Real violence cannot be limited to and contained by the specular relationship to sexual excitement; it exceeds representation. Pornography — with some exceptions — limits one to the image, the performance, the simulated deed. Pornographic excitement may be an attenuated use not only of symbolization but also of the transitional space. It forecloses the space between symbol and object and makes the represented object appear to be the "thing" that evokes excitement, but the thing is precisely not real. In pornographic sex, fantasies are not contained as symbolic representations in the subject's mind, they are routed via symbolic equation from the object directly to physical discharge. But the sexual act that brings about the discharge (most commonly, masturbation) is seldom a replica of the image that generates the excitement.

Speaking more generally, what does this analysis of attenuated symbolization say about the sadistic content of pornography and the proximity of aggression and sexuality? As I concluded in my discussion of omnipotence in Chapter 3, the point cannot be to "get rid of" dangerous fantasies; rather, it must be to contain and transform them through symbolization in the intersubjective space. By the same logic, my aim here is not to analyze sadism as if it were primarily or exclusively the property of pornographic fantasy — for we have already seen that aggression and fantasmatization are constitutive of sexual life. Rather, the point might be to distinguish between pornographic representation, which operates on the level of the symbolic equation, and forms of expression that provide fuller symbolic representation. In effect, while symbolization promotes the movement outward — the vector toward exchange with the outside (whether interpersonal communication or artistic sublimation) — the symbolic equation maintains the inward movement of fantasmatization, in which only discharge allows release.

We may now return to the question raised by the shared confrontation with the abyss, the gulf that separates one subject from another. In effect, it is the acceptance of this separation that makes shared contemplation possible, and it is with this acceptance that the erotic, the outward vector, is associated. Still, having seen the role of sexual fantasmatization in pornography, we might wish to know how "the sexual" and the erotic come together. Once we accept Laplanche's idea of the simultaneous formation of "the sexual," fantasy, and the unconscious, we cannot assume that there is any sexuality, any erotic relation, free of them. Rather (and this is the essence of what Freud discovered), sexuality — as a major dimension of the psyche — is necessarily imbued with and constituted by the fantasmic elements of "the sexual."

This understanding allows us to see that it is not simply the particular content of fantasy that makes some sexuality erotic and other sexuality pornographic. Certainly, the content of sexual fantasy is symptomatic of the way the problem of destruction has been shaped for the individual, of the vicissitudes of his self-other relations. But it is the relationship between the person and the fantasy, the fantasy and its form of expression, that makes the difference. Speaking more generally, what distinguishes the erotic — in interaction or representation — is the existence of an intersubjective space that both allows identification with the other and recognizes the non-identity between the person, the feeling, and the "thing" (action) representing it. We cannot say that sadomasochistic fantasy is inimical to or outside the erotic, for where do we find sexuality that is free of the fantasy of power and surrender? Would sexuality exist without such fantasy? There is no erotic interaction without the sense of self and other exerting power, affecting each other, and such affecting is immediately elaborated in the unconscious in the more violent terms of infantile sexuality. (E.g., a woman's fantasy of devouring her lover emerges in a dream, in which the visual image of a fox chasing a rabbit is followed by an auditory expression, the words said almost lovingly: "I'd like to drink your blood.") But what makes sexuality erotic is the survival of the other throughout the exercise of power, which in turn makes the expression of power part of symbolic play.

Eros can play with, rather than be extinguished by, the destruction wrought by fantasy: when the experience of union (fantasized, perhaps, as devouring or being consumed) can be contained symbolically and does not destroy the self; when sharing and attunement are not destroyed ("ruined" or "spoiled") by the other's outsideness and difference; when separate minds can share similar feelings. Eros unites us and in this sense overcomes the sense of otherness that afflicts the self in relation to the world and its own body. But this transcendence is possible only when one simultaneously recognizes the separateness of some outside body in all its particular sensuality, with all its particular difference.

Perhaps the origins of the erotic can be located before or beyond fantasy in the the simple corporeal sensuality and attunement central to the presymbolic world of the infant, the world illuminated first by intersubjective theory. The earliest mutual attunement of infant facial and kinetic play already creates an in-between space where two dance to the music of one, a precursor of the symbolic space of communicative play. The erotic pleasures of infancy predate the symbolic ability to equate one thing with another, to displace endlessly, which after all is the premise of the fantasmatizing of "the sexual." But the presymbolic life necessarily gives way to the symbolic world in which we are able to identify with actions and figures far beyond

the concrete by making links between distant and distinct en-
tities, to connect far-reaching effects. This expansion of the
world's impact on the mind is safe and enriching only when the
external is sufficiently differentiated from the internal, when
there is a usable outside other: nonretaliatory but able to be
affected, even hurt. Otherwise, the symbolic capacity produces a
threatening world of uncontrollable impingement by far-flung
causes, coercive "things," impervious objects, all indistinguishable embodiments of inexpressible, unprocessed material.

If real others actually engage in violent, traumatizing acts,
then the symbolic capacity becomes our worst nightmare. Only
when real others survive without retaliating, let alone attacking,
is there safety in the potential space of symbolization. Only
then is there sufficient separation between the object and our
reaction to it, and only then does symbolization free us from the
concrete. Otherwise the widening of our identifications stops
short of full symbolism and remains in the stage of symbolic
equations, in which the symbol is the thing symbolized. This
leads not to freedom but to the danger that images come alive,
symbolic "things," will make us feel without even touching us.
In such a world of demonic objects, sexuality can appear to be a
devil; it becomes a terrifying force through which, as MacKinnon implies, we can be made to do anything — compelled to
submit to destruction or to destroy in order to be rid of dangerous impulses that find no symbolic space for expression.

Not the violence of the images themselves but the closing
of the space between the object and its representation in order
to compel a reaction makes the pornographic different from full
symbolizing.[7] The whole point of pornography is to *make* you

7. What I mean by "full symbolizing" would not, I think, correspond to
Lacan's symbolic order alone, but to an integration of the Imaginary with the
Symbolic, which recognizes the origins of the latter in the former and allows the
transition from one to the other to be a "useful" space.

feel excited ("the devil made me do it"). The reduction of the symbolic to "things" that are identical with the symbols — "sex is violence" — captures both the pornographers and their opponents in the world of frightening objects. Ironically, then, pornographers appeal to a right of free expression that they cannot exercise; their form of revolt against inhibition reaffirms the very lack of freedom for symbolic, erotic play. However, to the extent that the antipornographers deny the distinction between pornography and symbolic play in artistic representation — a distinction that lies not in content but in form — they share the view of a psychic world of coercive forces, in which objects incarnate rather than symbolize power.

The fantasmic turning inward that makes aggression into its counterpart, "the sexual," can be experienced as benign only in the space of intersubjectivity, whether with a real or an imagined other. But as Segal (1957) herself points out, the line between symbolic equations and symbolization is a continuum, not a boundary. The distinction between fantasmic sexuality and symbolic play of eros is only a conceptual one. For in "real" sexual life, the distinction between the sexual and the erotic is not so easily upheld. In the abstract, we can agree with Freud that Eros is directed outward, toward the other; this places Eros in opposition to the turning inward of the sexual. For the sexual is the turning away from the world and even from one's own body sensuality, both of which become absorbed in the process of fantasmatization. Ever ambiguous, sexuality at once expresses this process and forms the most powerful conduit of erotic desire, desire for the other.

We could consider the distinction between the sexual and Eros as coincident with two hypothetical poles of sexuality, the one aligned with omnipotence, death, and fantasy, the other with recognition, life, and reality. Yet to this we would have to object that, as Freud says, Eros and death seldom appear sepa-rately. Thus, the converse of his conclusion is also true: that what we know about Eros is often what presents itself to us alloyed with its opposite — death, the destructive impulse.

For the idea of an object that can survive destruction also provides that destruction must have its say, that fantasy must endeavor to devour reality in order for the subject to taste the difference between them. And reality must survive the devour-ing of the unconscious in order to be more than mere repression, and thus to truly include the discovery of an other. Furthermore, the idea of the destruction of the object suggests the indispens-able role of aggression or negation in the subject's effort to reach another. The underlying argument about pornography and vio-lence among feminists is as much about the necessity, the place, of aggression as it is about sexuality. The antipornographers are in combat with aggression, they disavow it, they wish it to belong to men. They are not aware that disowning aggression means never tasting the difference, never giving up omnipotence, re-maining in the internal world of "subjective conceived" fantasy objects. Of course, the conscious and unconscious effort is to stay connected to the idealized good object, the good mother, nature. But only a good that survives hate can be experienced as an unthreatened, unprecarious good, and thus not requiring constant defense. For without successful destruction there can be no escape from the realm of idealization and fantasy, and hence no sexuality that is not literal and concrete, in its own way captive to the symbolic equation as much as pornography; no sexuality that includes recognition, and so no confrontation with difference and outsideness that is not violent and traumatic.

In intersubjective terms, aggression can be seen as an affect that becomes linked to one manifestation of a primary direction of the self. Aggression, like sexuality (before it becomes "the sexual"), is a given (and in that sense a *Trieb*), a blind motoric impulse.[8] The two become intertwined in the sexual. But aggression also, perhaps first, participates in destruction or negation: the moment of self-assertion, directed toward the other, the counterpart to recognition. Any act of the subject toward the other that has an impact "negates" the other, breaks into the other's absolute identity with her- or himself in such a way that the other is no longer exactly what she or he was a moment before. This change in the other constitutes the recognition the subject seeks — it can be sufficient to satisfy the aggressive tension.

This process of negation, acting on the other, and being recognized — Winnicott's destruction with survival — is initially the opposite of the turning in on the self. Negation, I have argued, is usually directed first toward the other and becomes internalized only when the other cannot receive or transmute or contain, above all recognize, the subject's act. In erotic exchange, the other *does* receive and recognize the impact of the subject. If "the sexual" arises as the negative of Eros, it is because Eros — the striving toward the other, the process of recognition — cannot succeed alone in containing all aggression; some must turn inward to evolve within the sphere of omnipotence.

Aggression, like sexuality, is thus not necessarily associated

8. This is actually a far more complicated problem because aggression almost never appears as simply peremptory (S. Mitchell 1993) but as reactive or intertwined with complex fantasies. What I mean here is that the common confusion about motoric discharge and aggression is not accidental: there appears to be some tension that has to find discharge through affecting the other, and thus is always aimed at an object. Is it the aim, or the impediment to the aim, that entitles us to call it aggression? In Winnicott's (1989) reflections on destruction he comments that the "destructive" (fire-air or other) aliveness of the individual is simply a symptom of being alive. He compares aggression to fire, a force like outbreathing, quoting Pliny: "Who can say whether in essence fire is constructive or destructive?" Through Winnicott might we arrive at a more liberal reading of Freud, in which we call this tension aggression but differentiate creative and destructive aims, aims that reach their intersubjective target and aims that do not?

with death or even with "the sexual" but can serve more than one master. As the inextricable counterpoint to recognition, destruction is not the negation of Eros but its complement. Thus Eros cannot, need not, evade aggression, which so often fuels destructiveness. Rather, we might rethink Freud's remark at the close of *Civilization and Its Discontents*, that "now it is to be expected that the other of the two 'Heavenly Powers,' eternal Eros, will make an effort to assert himself in the struggle with his equally immortal adversary" (p. 145). Because there can be no useful experience of destruction and survival without aggression, the question is really how its immortal adversary, Eros, can inspire aggression to assume its most creative form, destruction survived. In light of Freud and Bataille, we might say that when it is allied with Eros, destruction helps us to cross the sea of death that separates us. The task of Eros may be, then, to summon back to the "Heavenly Powers" its cast off foe, "the spirit that negates (Der Geist der stets verneint)," who is, as Goethe's Mephistopheles tells us, "Part of that force which would / Do evil evermore, and yet creates the good (Ein Teil von jener Kraft, / Die stets das Böse will und stets das Gute Schafft)."

References

Abelin, E. L. 1980. Triangulation, the role of the father and the origins of core gender identity during the rapprochement subphase. In *Rapprochement*, ed. R. F. Lax, S. Bach, and J. A. Burland, 151–170. New York: Aronson.

Aron, L. 1992. Interpretation as the expression of the analyst's subjectivity. *Psychoanal. Dial.* 2:475–508.

———. 1995. The internalized primal scene. *Psychoanal. Dial.* 5:195–237.

Atwood, G., and R. Stolorow. 1984. *Structures of subjectivity.* Hillsdale, N.J.: Analytic Press.

Bassin, D. 1994. Beyond the he and she: Postoedipal transcendence of gender polarities. *J. Amer. Psychoanal. Assoc.* (forthcoming).

Bataille, G. 1962. *Death and sensuality.* New York: Walker.

———. 1976. Hegel in the light of Hemingway. *Semiotexte* 2:2–22.

———. 1985. *Visions of excess: Selected writings, 1927–1939*, ed. A. Stoekl. Minneapolis: University of Minnesota Press.

de Beauvoir, S. *The Second Sex.* New York: Knopf, 1952.

Beebe, B. 1985. Mother-infant mutual influence and precursors of self and object representations. In *Empirical studies of psychoanalytic theories.* Vol. 2, ed. J. Masling, 27–48. Hillsdale, N.J.: Analytic Press.

Beebe, B., and F. Lachmann. 1988. The contribution of mother-infant mutual influence to the origins of self and object representations. *Psychoanal. Psychol.* 5:305–337.

———. 1994. Representation and internalization in infancy: Three principles of salience. *Psychoanal. Psychol.* 11:127–165.

Beebe, B., and D. Stern. 1977. Engagement-disengagement and early object experiences. In *Communicative structures and psychic structures*, ed. N. Freedman and S. Grand. New York: Plenum.

Benhabib, S. 1995. Feminism and postmodernism. In *Feminist contentions: A philosophical exchange*, 17–34. New York: Routledge.

Benjamin, J. 1980. The bonds of love: Erotic domination and rational violence. In *The future of difference*, ed. H. Eisenstein and A. Jardine. Boston, G. K. Hall.

———. 1986. The alienation of desire: Woman's masochism and ideal love. In *Psychoanalysis and women: Contemporary reappraisals*, ed. J. Alpert, 113–138. Hillsdale, N.J.: Analytic Press.

———. 1988. *The bonds of love: Psychoanalysis, feminism, and the problem of domination*. New York: Pantheon.

———. 1990. An outline of intersubjectivity. *Psychoanal. Psychol.* 7, supplement, 33–46.

———. 1991. Father and daughter: Identification with difference — a contribution to gender heterodoxy. *Psychoanal. Dial.* 1:277–299.

———. 1994. The shadow of the other (subject): Intersubjectivity and feminist theory. *Constellations* 1, no. 2, 231–254.

Bernheimer, C., and C. Kahane, eds. 1985. *In Dora's case: Freud-hysteria-feminism.* New York: Columbia University Press.

Bernstein, D. 1983. The female superego: A different perspective. *Internat. J. Psychoanal.* 64:187–202.

Bion, W. 1962a. A theory of thinking. *Internat. J. Psychoanal.* 43:306–310. Rpt. in *Melanie Klein Today.* Vol. 1, ed. E. Bott-Spilius, 178–186. London: Routledge, 1988.

———. 1962b. *Learning from experience.* In *Seven servants.* New York: Aronson, 1977.

Blos, P. 1984. Son and father. *J. Amer. Psychoanal. Assoc.* 32:301–324.

Bollas, C. 1987. *The shadow of the object; Psychoanalysis of the unthought known.* London: Free Association.

———. 1989. *Forces of destiny: Psychoanalysis and human idiom.* London: Free Association.

———. 1992. *Being a character: Psychoanalysis and self experience.* New York: Hill and Wang.

Borch-Jacobsen, R. 1988. *The Freudian subject.* Stanford: Stanford University Press.

Brennan, T. 1992. *The interpretation of the flesh.* New York: Routledge.

Bromberg, P. 1993. Shadow and substance: A relational perspective on clinical process. *Psychoanal. Psychol.* 10, no. 2, 147–168.

Butler, J. 1990. *Gender trouble.* New York: Routledge.

———. 1994. Poststructuralism and postmarxism. *Diacritics* 23, no. 4, 3–11.

———. 1995. Melancholy gender/refused identification. *Psych. Dial.* 5.

Chasseguet-Smirgel, J. 1970. Feminine guilt and the Oedipus complex. In *Female sexuality: New psychoanalytic views,* ed. J. Chasseguet-Smirgel, 94–134. Ann Arbor: University of Michigan Press.

———. 1976. Freud and female sexuality. *Internat. J. Psychoanal.* 57:275–286.

———. 1984. *Creativity and Perversion.* New York: Norton.

———. 1985. *The ego ideal: A psychoanalytic essay on the malady of the ideal.* New York: Norton.

Chodorow, N. 1978. *The reproduction of mothering.* Berkeley: University of California Press.

———. 1979. Gender, relations and difference in psychoanalytic perspective. In *Feminism and psychoanalytic theory.* New Haven: Yale University Press, 1989.

———. 1992. Heterosexuality as a compromise formation: Reflections on the psychoanalytic theory of sexual development. *Psychoanal. and Contemp. Thought* 15:267–304.

Chodorow, N., and S. Contratto. 1982. The fantasy of the perfect mother. In *Feminism and psychoanalytic theory.* New Haven: Yale University Press, 1989.

Christiansen, A. 1993. Masculinity and its vicissitudes. Paper presented at Seminar on Psychoanalysis and Sexual Difference, New York, Institute for the Humanities.

Clower, V. L. 1977. Theoretical implications in current views of masturbation in latency girls. In *Female psychology,* ed. H. Blum, 109–126. New York: International Universities Press.

Coates, S., R. Friedman, and S. Wolfe. 1991. The etiology of boyhood gender disorder. *Psychoanal. Dial.* 1:481–524.

Cornell, D. 1992. *The philosophy of the limit.* New York: Routledge.

Culler, J. 1982. *On deconstruction: Theory and criticism after structuralism.* Ithaca: Cornell University Press.

Davies, J. 1994. Love in the afternoon: A relational consideration of desire and dread in the countertransference. *Psychoanal. Dial.* 4:153–170.

Davies, J., and M. Frawley. 1993. *Treating the adult survivor of childhood sexual abuse.* New York: Basic.

De Lauretis, T. 1994. *The practice of love: Lesbian sexuality and perverse desire.* Bloomington: Indiana University Press.

Derrida, J. 1976. *Of grammatology.* Trans. G. Spivak. Baltimore: Johns Hopkins University Press.

———. 1978. *Writing and difference.* Trans. A. Bass. Chicago: University of Chicago Press.

———. 1982. *Margins of philosophy.* Trans. A. Bass. Chicago: University of Chicago Press.

Dimen, M. 1991. Deconstructing difference: Gender, splitting, and transitional space. *Psychoanal. Dial.* 1:335–352.

Dinnerstein, D. 1976. *The Mermaid and the Minotaur.* New York: Harper and Row.

Dworkin, A. 1980. Pornography and grief. In *Take back the night*, ed. L. Lederer. New York: William Morrow.

Eagle, M. 1984. *Recent developments in psychoanalysis: A critical evaluation.* Cambridge: Harvard University Press.

Eigen, M. 1981. The area of faith in Winnicott, Lacan and Bion. *Internat. J. Psychoanal.* 62:413–433.

———. 1991. Winnicott's area of freedom: The uncompromisable. In *Liminality and transitional phenomena*, ed. N. Schwartz-Salant and M. Stern. Wilmette, Ill.: Chiron.

———. 1993. *The electrified tightrope.* Northvale, N.J.: Aronson.

Eliot, George. 1871. *Middlemarch.* Harmondsworth: Penguin, 1965.

Fast, I. 1984. *Gender identity.* Hillsdale, N.J.: Analytic Press.

———. 1990. Aspects of early gender development: Toward a reformulation. *Psychoanal. Psychol.* 7, supplement, 105–118.

First, E. 1988. The leaving game: I'll play you and you'll play me; the emergence of the capacity for dramatic role play in two-year-olds. In *Modes of meaning: Clinical and developmental approaches to symbolic play*, ed. A. Slade and D. Wolfe, 132–160. New York: Oxford University Press.

———. 1994. Mothering, hate, and Winnicott. In *Representations of motherhood*, ed. D. Bassin, M. Honey, and M. Kaplan, 147–161. New Haven: Yale University Press.

Flax, J. 1990. *Thinking fragments: Psychoanalysis, feminism, and post-modernism in the contemporary West.* Los Angeles: University of California Press.

Foucault, M. 1972. *The archaeology of knowledge.* Trans. A. M. Sheridan Smith. New York: Pantheon.

———. 1977. What is an author? In *Language, counter-memory and practice,* ed. D. Bouchard. Trans. D. Bouchard and S. Simon. Ithaca: Cornell University Press.

———. 1980. *The history of sexuality.* Vol. 1, *An introduction.* Trans. J. R. Hurley. New York: Random House.

Freedman, N. 1980. On splitting and its resolution. *Psychoanal. and Contemp. Thought,* 3:237–66.

Freud, S. 1911. Formulation on the two principles in mental functioning. *Standard Edition* 12:213–226. London: Hogarth, 1958.

———. 1912a. The dynamics of transference. *SE* 12:97–107. London: Hogarth, 1958.

———. 1912b. Recommendations to physicians practicing psychoanalysis. *SE* 12:109–120. London: Hogarth, 1958.

———. 1914. On narcissism: An introduction. *SE* 14:67–102. London: Hogarth, 1958.

———. 1915a. Instincts and their vicissitudes. *SE* 14:109–140. London: Hogarth, 1958.

———. 1915b. Observations on transference love. *SE* 12:157–171. London: Hogarth, 1958.

———. 1919. "A child is being beaten." *SE* 17:179–204. London: Hogarth, 1955.

———. 1920. Beyond the pleasure principle. *SE* 18:7–64. London: Hogarth, 1955.

———. 1921. Group psychology and the analysis of the ego. *SE* 18:67–144. London: Hogarth, 1955.

———. 1923. The ego and the id. *SE* 19:1–66. London: Hogarth, 1961.

———. 1924a. The economic problem of masochism. *SE* 19:159–172. London: Hogarth, 1961.

———. 1924b. The dissolution of the Oedipus complex. *SE* 19:173–182. London: Hogarth, 1961.

———. 1925. Some psychical consequences of the anatomical distinction between the sexes. *SE* 19:248–260. London: Hogarth, 1961.

———. 1930. Civilization and its discontents. *SE* 23:. London: Hogarth, 1953.

———. 1931. Female sexuality. *SE* 21:225–246. London: Hogarth, 1961.

———. 1933. New introductory lectures on psychoanalysis: Femininity. *SE* 22:112–135. London: Hogarth, 1961.

Fuss, D. 1989. *Essentially speaking: Feminism, nature, and difference.* New York: Routledge.

Galenson, E., and H. Roiphe. 1982. The preoedipal relationship of a father, mother, and daughter. In *Father and child*, ed. S. H. Cath, A. R. Gurwitt, and J. M. Ross, 151–162. Boston: Little, Brown.

Gallop, J. 1982. *The daughter's seduction: Feminism and psychoanalysis.* Ithaca: Cornell University Press.

———. 1989. The monster in the mirror: The feminist critic's psychoanalysis. In *Feminism and psychoanalysis*, ed. R. Feldstein and J. Roof, 13–24. Ithaca: Cornell University Press.

Ghent, E. 1989. Credo: The dialectics of one-person and two-person psychologies. *Contemp. Psychoanal.* 25:169–211.

———. 1990. Masochism, submission, surrender. *Contemp. Psychoanal.* 26:108–136.

Gilligan, C. 1982. *In a different voice.* Cambridge: Harvard University Press.

Goldner, V. 1991. Toward a critical relational theory of gender. *Psychoanal. Dial.* 1:249–272.

Gornick, L. 1986. Developing a new narrative: The woman therapist and the male patient. In *Women and psychoanalysis: Contemporary reappraisals*, ed. J. Alpert, 257–286. Hillsdale, N.J.: Analytic Press.

Green, A. 1986. The analyst, symbolization, and absence in the analytic setting. In *On private madness.* New York: International Universities Press.

Greenberg, J., and S. Mitchell. 1983. *Object relations in psychoanalytic theory.* Cambridge: Harvard University Press.

Greenson, R. 1968. Dis-identifying from mother: Its special importance for the boy. *Internat. J. Psychoanal.* 49:370–374.

Grossman, W. I., and W. A. Stewart. 1977. Penis envy: From childhood wish to developmental metaphor. In *Female psychology*, ed. H. Blum, 193–212. New York: International Universities Press.

Gunsberg, L. 1982. Selected critical review of psychological investigations of the early father-infant relationship. In *Father and child,* ed. S. H. Cath, A. R. Gurwitt, and J. M. Ross, 65–82. Boston: Little, Brown.

Habermas, J. 1970. A theory of communicative competence. In *Recent sociology*. No. 2, ed. H. P. Dreitzel. New York: Macmillan.

——. 1971. *Knowledge and human interests*. Boston: Beacon.

——. 1992. Individuation through socialization: Meade's theory of subjectivity. In *Postmetaphysical thinking*. Cambridge: M.I.T. University Press.

Harris, A. 1991. Gender as contradiction: A discussion of Freud's "The psychogenesis of a case of homosexuality in a woman." *Psychoanal. Dial.* 2:197–224.

Herman, J. 1992. *Trauma and recovery*. New York: Basic.

Hill, D. 1994. The special place of the erotic transference in psychoanalysis. *Psychoanal. Inq.* 14:483–498.

Hirsch, I. 1994. Counter-transference love and theoretical model. Psychoanalytic Dialogues 4, no. 2, 171–192.

Hoffman, I. 1983. The patient as interpreter of the analyst's experience. *Contemp. Psychoanal.* 19:389–422.

——. 1991. Discussion: Toward a social-constructivist view of the psychoanalytic situation. *Psychoanal. Dial.* 1:74–105.

——. 1994. Dialectical thinking and therapeutic action in the psychoanalytic process. *Psychoanal. Q.* 63:187–218.

Hollibaugh, A., and C. Moraga. 1983. What we're rolling around in bed with: Sexual silences in feminism. In *Powers of desire*, ed. A. Snitow, C. Stansell, and S. Thompson, 394–405. New York: Monthly Review.

Honneth, A. 1992. *Kampf um Anerkennung*. Frankfurt: Suhrkamp.

Horkheimer, M., and T. Adorno. 1947. *Dialectic of enlightenment*. New York: Seabury, 1972.

Horney, K. 1924. On the genesis of the castration complex in women. In *Feminine psychology*, 37–54. New York: Norton, 1967.

——. 1926. The flight from womanhood. In *Feminine psychology*, 55–70. New York: Norton, 1967.

——. 1932. The dread of woman. In *Feminine psychology*, 133–146. New York: Norton, 1967.

——. 1933a. The denial of the vagina. In *Feminine psychology*, 147–162. New York: Norton, 1967.

——. 1933b. The problem of feminine masochism. In *Feminine psychology*, 214–233. New York: Norton, 1967.

Irigaray, L. 1985. *Speculum of the other woman.* Trans. G. Gill. Ithaca: Cornell University Press.

———. 1991. The bodily encounter with the mother. In *The Irigaray reader,* ed. M. Whitford, 34–46. Oxford: Basil Blackwell.

Jacobson, E. 1937. Ways of female superego formation and the female castration conflict. *Psychoanal. Q.* 45 (1976):525–538.

Jones, E. 1927. Early development of female sexuality. In *Papers on psychoanalysis.* Boston: Beacon, 1961.

———. 1933. Early female sexuality. In *Papers on psychoanalysis.* Boston: Beacon, 1961.

Kernberg, O. 1991. Aggression and love in the relationship of the couple. *J. Amer. Psychoanal. Assoc.* 39:45–70.

Khan, M. 1979. *Alienation in perversions.* New York: International Universities Press.

Klein, M. 1928. Early states of the Oedipus complex. *Internat. J. Psychoanal.* 9:167–180.

———. 1945. The Oedipus complex in light of early anxieties. In *Contributions to Psycho-Analysis, 1921–1945.* London: Hogarth, 1948.

Kohut H. 1977. *The restoration of the self.* New York: International Universities Press.

———. 1984. *How does analysis cure?* Chicago: University of Chicago Press.

Kramer, S. 1994. Betwixt the dark and the daylight. Paper presented at Seminar on Psychoanalysis and Sexual Difference, New York, Institute for the Humanities.

Kristeva, J. 1981. Women's time. *Signs* 7:13–35.

———. 1986. Stabat mater. In *The Kristeva reader,* ed. T. Moi, 160–185. New York: Columbia University Press.

———. 1987. Freud and love. In *Tales of love.* New York: Columbia University Press.

———. 1991. *Strangers to ourselves.* New York: Columbia University Press.

Lacan, J. 1949. The mirror stage as formative of the function of the I. In *Ecrits: A selection.* New York: Norton, 1977.

———. 1982. Intervention on the transference. In *Feminine sexuality: Jacques Lacan and the école freudienne,* ed. J. Mitchell and J. Rose, 61–73. New York: Norton.

Lachmann, F. 1986. Interpretation of psychic conflict and adversarial relationships: A self psychological perspective. *Psychoanal. Psychol.* 3:341–355.

———. 1994. How can I eroticize thee? Let me count the ways. *Psychoanal. Inq.* 14:604–621.

Lamb, M. E. 1977. The development of parental preferences in the first two years of life. *Sex Roles* 3:495–497.

Laplanche, J. 1976. *Life and death in psychoanalysis.* Baltimore: Johns Hopkins University Press.

Laplanche, J., and J. Pontalis. 1973. *The language of psychoanalysis.* New York: Norton.

Lax, R. 1977. The role of internalization in the development of certain aspects of female masochism: Ego psychological considerations. *Internat. J. Psychoanal.* 58:289–300.

Lazarre, J. 1991. *Worlds beyond my control.* New York: Viking.

Lester, E. 1985. The female analyst and the erotized transference. *Internat. J. Psychoanal.* 66:283–293.

Levenson, R. 1984. Intimacy, autonomy and gender: Developmental differences and their reflection in adult relationships. *J. Am. Acad. Psychoanal.* 12:529–544.

Loewald, H. 1980. Ego and reality. In *Papers on psychoanalysis,* 3–20. New Haven: Yale University Press.

MacDougall, J. 1980. *Plea for a measure of abnormality.* New York: International Universities Press.

MacKinnon, C. 1987. *Feminism unmodified: Discourses on life and law.* Cambridge: Harvard University Press.

Mahler, M., F. Pine, and A. Bergman. 1975. *The psychological birth of the human infant.* New York: Basic.

Marcuse, H. 1962. *Eros and civilization.* New York: Vintage.

Martin, B. 1982. Feminism, criticism, and Foucault. *New German Critique* 27:3–30.

May, R. 1986. Concerning a psychoanalytic view of maleness. *Psychoanal. Rev.* 73:175–193.

Mayer, E. 1985. Everybody must be like me. *Internat. J. Psychoanal.* 66:331–348.

Meehan, J. 1994. Autonomy, recognition and respect: Habermas, Benjamin, Honneth. *Constellations* 1, no. 2, 270–285.

Milner, M. 1952. The role of illusion in symbol formation. In Milner 1987, 83–113. London: Tavistock, 1987.

———. 1957. The ordering of chaos. In Milner 1987, 216–233. London: Tavistock, 1987.

———. 1987. *The suppressed madness of sane men*. London: Tavistock.

Mitchell, J. 1974. *Psychoanalysis and feminism*. New York: Pantheon.

———. 1982. Introduction. *Feminine sexuality: Jacques Lacan and the école freudienne*, ed. J. Mitchell and J. Rose, 1–26. New York: Norton.

Mitchell, S. 1988. *Relational concepts in psychoanalysis*. Cambridge: Harvard University Press.

———. 1993. *Hope and dread in psychoanalysis*. New York: Basic.

Modell, A. 1984. *Psychoanalysis in a new context*. New York: International Universities Press.

Nicholson, L. 1990. *Feminism/postmodernism*. New York: Routledge.

Ogden, T. 1986. *The matrix of the mind*. New York: Aronson.

———. 1987. The transitional Oedipal relationship in female development. *Internat. J. Psychoanal.* 68:485–498.

Person, E. 1985. The erotic transference in women and men: Differences and consequences. *J. Amer. Acad. of Psychoanal.* 13, no. 2, 159–180.

———. 1988. *Dreams of love and fateful encounters*. New York: Norton.

Person, E., and L. Ovesey. 1983. Psychoanalytic theories of gender identity. *J. Amer. Acad. Psychoanal.* 11:203–226.

Pizer, S. 1992. The negotiation of paradox in the analytic process. *Psychoanal. Dial.* 2:215–240.

Pruett, K. 1987. *The nurturing father*. New York: Warner.

Ragland-Sullivan, E. 1986. *Jacques Lacan and the philosophy of psychoanalysis*. Urbana: University of Illinois Press.

Reage, P. 1965. *Story of O*. New York: Grove.

Reich, A. 1940. A contribution to the psychoanalysis of extreme submissiveness in women. *Psychoanal. Q.* 9:470–480.

Riley, D. 1988. *"Am I that name?" Feminism and the category of woman in history*. London: Macmillan.

Rilke, R. M. 1939. *Duino elegies*. Trans. J. B. Leishman and S. Spender. New York: Norton, 1963.

Rivera, M. 1989. Linking the psychological and the social: Feminism, poststructuralism and multiple personality. *Dissociation* 2, no. 1, 24–31.

Roiphe, H., and E. Galenson. 1981. *Infantile origins of sexual identity*. New York: International Universities Press.

Rose, J. 1982. Introduction 2 to *Feminine sexuality: Jacques Lacan and the école freudienne*, ed. J. Mitchell and J. Rose. New York: Norton.

———. 1986. *Sexuality in the field of vision*. London: Verso.

Ruddick, S. 1989. *Maternal thinking*. Boston: Beacon.

Sander, L. 1983. Polarity, paradox, and the organizing process in development. In *Frontiers of infant psychiatry*. No. 1, ed. J. D. Call, E. Galenson, and R. L. Tyson, 333–346. New York: Basic.

Sandler, J. 1993. On communication from patient to analyst: Not everything is projective identification. *Internat. J. of Psychoanal.* 74:1097–1109.

Santner, E. 1990. *Stranded objects*. Ithaca: Cornell University Press.

Schachtel, Z. 1986. The impossible profession. In *Psychoanalysis and women: Contemporary reappraisals*, ed. J. Alpert, 237–256. Hillsdale, N.J.: Analytic Press.

Scott, J. 1988. *Gender and the politics of history*. New York: Columbia University Press.

———. 1993. The tip of the volcano. *J. Soc. Comp. Study of Society and History* 5:438–457.

Segal, H. 1957. Notes on symbol formation. *Internat. J. Psychoanal.* 38:391–397.

Sheperdson, C. 1993. Image, mother, woman: Lacan and Kristeva. Paper presented at Conference on the Object, SUNY-Buffalo.

Skolnick, N., and S. Warshaw. 1993. *Relational perspectives in psychoanalysis*. Hillsdale, N.J.: Analytic Press.

Spezzano, C. 1993. *Affect in psychoanalysis: A clinical synthesis*. Hillsdale, N.J.: Analytic Press.

———. 1994. Affects, object relations, and intersubjectivity: Toward a new American "Middle School" theory of mind. Paper presented at National Institute for the Psychotherapies, New York.

Spieler, S. 1984. Preoedipal girls need fathers. *Psychoanal. Rev.* 71:63–80.

Sprengnether, M. 1990. *The spectral mother: Freud, feminism, and psychoanalysis*. Ithaca: Cornell University Press.

———. 1995. Reading Freud's life. *American Imago* 52:9–54.

Stern, D. 1974. The goal and structure of mother-infant play. *J. Amer. Acad. Child Psychiatry* 13:402–421.

———. 1977. *The first relationship: Infant and mother*. Cambridge: Harvard University Press.

———. 1985. *The interpersonal world of the infant.* New York: Basic.

Stern, D. B. 1992. Commentary of constructivism in clinical psychoanalysis. *Psychoanal. Dial.* 2:331–364.

Stoller, R. J. 1968. *Sex and gender.* New York: Aronson.

———. 1973. Facts and fancies: An examination of Freud's concept of bisexuality. In *Women and analysis,* ed. J. Strouse, 340–363. Boston: G. K. Hall, 1985.

———. 1975. *Perversion: The erotic form of hatred.* New York: Pantheon.

———. 1980. *Sexual excitement.* New York: Simon and Schuster.

———. 1985. *Observing the erotic imagination.* New Haven: Yale University Press.

Stolorow, R. 1986. On experiencing an object: A multidimensional perspective. In *Progress in self psychology.* Vol. 2, ed. A. Goldberg, 273–279. New York: Guilford.

Stolorow, R., B. Brandchaft, and G. Atwood. 1987. *Psychoanalytic treatment: An intersubjective approach.* Hillsdale, N.J.: Analytic Press.

Stolorow, R., and F. Lachmann. 1980. *Psychoanalysis of developmental arrest.* New York: International Universities Press.

Suleiman, S. 1985. Writing and motherhood. In *The (m)other tongue,* ed. C. Kahane, S. Garner, and M. Sprengnether, 352–377. Ithaca: Cornell University Press.

———. 1988. On maternal splitting: A propos of Mary Gordon's *Men and angels. Signs* 14:25–41.

———. 1990. Feminist intertexuality and the laugh of the mother. In *Subversive intent.* Cambridge: Harvard University Press.

Thurman. J. 1981. *Isak Dinesen: The life of a storyteller.* New York: St. Martin's.

Trevarthen, C. 1980. The foundations of intersubjectivity: The development of interpersonal and cooperative understanding in infants. In *The social foundations of language and thought,* ed. D. R. Olson. New York: Norton.

Tronick, E. 1989. Emotions and emotional communication in infants. *Amer. Psychologist* 44, no. 2, 112–119.

Tyson, P. 1986. Male gender identity: Early developmental roots. *Psychoanal. Rev.* 73:405–425.

Welles, J., and H. K. Wrye. 1991. The maternal erotic transference. *Internat. J. Psychoanal.* 72:93–106.

Whitebook, J. 1994. Hypostatizing Thanatos: Lacan's analysis of the ego. *Constellations* 1, no. 2, 214–230.

Winnicott, D. W. 1947. Hate in the countertransference. In *Through pediatrics to psychoanalysis.* New York: Basic, 1975.

———. 1960. Ego distortion in terms of true and false self. In *The maturational process and the facilitating environment.* New York: International Universities Press

———. 1964. *The child, the family and the outside world.* Harmondsworth, U.K.: Penguin.

———. 1969a. Creativity and its origins. In *Playing and reality,* 76–93. New York: Basic, 1971.

———. 1969b. The use of an object and relating through identification. In *Playing and reality,* 86–94. New York: Basic, 1971.

———. 1989. *Psychoanalytic explorations.* Cambridge: Harvard University Press.

Young-Bruehl, E. 1988. *Anna Freud.* New York: Summit.

Index